The Truth Behind Hip-hop

G. Craige Lewis

The Truth Behind Hip-hop
by G. Craige Lewis

Printed in the United States of America

ISBN 978-1-60791-916-2

www.xulonpress.com

This book is dedicated to the memory of my father
Elder G. L. Lewis. Miss you daddy.

Contents

Chapter 1

The Spirit of Hip-hop

Have you ever seen the Hollywood classic *King Kong*? It is amazing how this monstrous forty-foot ape was imported from Africa and expected to be controlled in New York City. In the 2006 remake, Kong is strapped down and apparently sedated, as this enormous beast was put on display to entertain thousands of people in a theater. The amused audience was shocked and surprised, however, when this monster broke from its restraints and began killing people, destroying lives, and tearing up New York City. Suddenly, the idea of "a big ape with a cute crush" wasn't funny anymore. Their dilemma was that they were trying to be entertained by a beast they could not control. Thankfully, Kong doesn't exist, but another monster does. The reality is that a spiritually imported, supernatural beast is destroying our nation today: hip-hop.

In this book, you will see how hip-hop is destroying the lives of many, as they seek to be entertained by a supernatural influence that is beyond their natural control. This would have been hard for me to believe had I not experienced it firsthand.

I can remember the first time I spoke the core message of EX Ministries. Back in 1996, I was asked to speak at a music crusade at the Texas Music Hall in Dallas. After a time of prayer and fasting, God prepared me to speak, but it was not for the message I had prepared. A little nervous because of the prominent people in the audience, I stood in the stage wings with my Bible and my notes in hand. Just when I was ready to preach what I had prepared, the inward voice of the Holy Spirit clearly said to me, "Talk about the music!"

I did not want to, honestly, because I had prepared something different. But the prompting from the Lord did not stop. I knew He was insisting that I speak about music and the plan of the enemy through hip-hop. I reluctantly walked out on stage and obeyed the voice of the Lord. Little did I know that my fasting and praying prepared me to release a message I had studied, but never before delivered. Emboldened by the presence of God, I released what He revealed to me. That night, I followed the Holy Spirit's leading during the entire message in a way that I had never done before. It was powerful!

Afterward, the people could not believe what they had just heard, but they knew it was truth from God. They were flabbergasted, and so was I! As I spoke, I was listening to myself, and even I was surprised by what I was saying! The Holy Spirit truly took over, and I was amazed at the power of this message and how it was delivered. Little did I know, that night God released the beginnings of a history-making message that would change lives for years to come, birthing EX Ministries and its core message, "The Truth Behind Hip-hop."

Backstage, we were eating and fellowshipping after the message was given, and a young man and his wife approached me. He introduced himself to me and said that he was Kevin and was part of a popular secular recording group called Color Me Badd. He began telling me how God used this message to change his mind about being in the group, and he wanted out. They were just about to sign another major contract with Sony, but he did not feel right about it anymore because of the message God gave me to speak that night. At that moment, I saw a glimpse of what God was doing. Though I knew God was introducing me to my calling, I did not know I was about to come face to face with the power of God and my nemesis: hip-hop. This was a divine setup! As I began to pray for Kevin, the power of God overwhelmed him, and he fell to his knees. God touched him and brought him out of darkness into His light. That night, Kevin met with the remaining members of the group and quit

Color Me Badd forever! But that is not the end of this story; it is just the beginning.

Kevin and I stayed good friends after that incident. We communicated and talked from time to time. But every now and then, I would lose contact with him, as if he was avoiding me at times. I could not really figure it out, but I knew there was something about the peculiar way he dodged me. Eventually, after not speaking for several months, I called him, and Kevin admitted he was avoiding me because he was about to pursue a publishing deal to write secular music. Now, most people know that I am straightforward, especially with my friends. After I spoke with him, he, of course, was mad, but he knew the Word of God was shared with him. He knew he could not turn around. Soon, Kevin was about to come face to face with the diabolical forces that were trying to pull him back.

Deliverance From Hip-Hop

A few weeks passed, and I got a call on a Friday night. Kevin called me and began to tell how he went to a Bob Larson Crusade, and was delivered from a demon spirit that was inside of him. Now, I know many of you may question whether or not a Christian can have a demon, and I questioned it myself. But whatever your theory or mine is on this matter, KEVIN HAD A DEMON! During his deliverance service, Bob walked over to where Kevin was sitting, and a demon began to manifest in Kevin. It identified itself as the spirit of wrath. Bob addressed the spirit and cast it out. Kevin was very excited on the phone that night when he talked about it. He could not believe that even after he had quit his group and pretty much changed his lifestyle, there could still be a spirit like that attached to him. More than likely, this spirit could no longer hide because of the presence of God and Kevin's obedience to make the changes God wanted in his life. After speaking with him that night, I got off the phone and went to bed. It turns out, however, that was not the end of this ordeal.

The next day, I was sitting in my recording studio, and I received a phone call from Kevin's wife, Tammie. She was very disturbed and could barely talk. She told me that Kevin was on his way home from work, and demons began to manifest in him. The spirits tried to cause him to crash his car as he drove home from work! She even put her cell phone, which Kevin was on, up to her home phone that I was on, and I could hear the evil spirits speaking through him. Tammie asked me to come over and minister to Kevin once he got home. I hesitated, but I agreed.

I then called my wife, who was out of town at the time, and I told her what was happening. I told her that I did not want to go, honestly, because I was scared to death! I had never dealt with demons, and I was not sure what to do, so I tried to discourage myself from going. But somehow, I ended up in my car, on my way over to Kevin's house. I even tried to get lost, but the Lord guided me there anyway. You better believe that I was praying and repenting all the way over! I did not know what to expect, or what to do.

As I drove up to Kevin's house, I could see through his front window, and I did not like what was going on inside. Frantically yelling, swearing, and supernaturally strong, Kevin was viciously wrestling with a couple of his church members. I stayed in my car, very apprehensive. I told the Holy Spirit, "I'm not going in there!" And the Holy Spirit spoke to me very plainly and said, "You are right. You are not going in there, as you. But you are going in, representing Me!" The Bible says:

> Finally, my brethren, be strong [not in yourself, but] *in the Lord*, and in the power of *his might [not your might]*.
> Ephesians 6:10, emphasis added

More confident because of the Lord's assurance, I got out of the car and walked up to the house. When I walked in the front door, the demon in Kevin looked at me and began to scream, "No, no, no, not him!" and the spirit caused Kevin to violently try to escape. I looked and was amazed at how afraid the demons in Kevin were of me. But the Holy Spirit spoke to me and told me, "They are not afraid of you; they are afraid of your assignment!" Of course, they were not afraid of me, but rather, the Christ in me. As the night progressed and I ministered deliverance to Kevin, I began to see how God had strategically placed Kevin in my life for me to experience this. I learned more about music, the devil, and the plan of the enemy from this deliverance than from all my years of study.

I began to deal with the evil spirits in Kevin, and time will not permit me to tell the whole story, but there are some very important things that I learned from Kevin's deliverance that I must share. Kevin's very popular group had a hit song called "I Wanna Sex You Up," which appeared in a movie called *New Jack City* and stayed near the top of the Billboard charts for weeks. Color Me Badd's album later went triple platinum. This song was very explicit, and the scene in the movie where the song is featured was explicit as well.

While praying for Kevin's deliverance that night, a spirit of witchcraft manifested through Kevin and began to speak. This demon told me that witches that cast spells on music summoned it, and other demons, into that song. Compelled by the Holy Spirit, this demon further revealed that their assignment for this song was to cause young girls to lose their virginity. I could not believe my ears! Then I remembered, back when the song was out, young guys told me that if you really wanted to get a girl to have sex with you, play "I Wanna Sex You Up"! They always said, "There's just something about that song!" Wow! Kevin even confirmed later how countless young girls told him they lost their virginity to this song! The plan of the enemy was revealed even more by the next demon that I faced in Kevin.

I was exhausted from hours of ministering to Kevin, and I sat down on the floor to rest. As I sat, an evil spirit manifested in Kevin and frowned at me. The demon said, "Wanna talk?" I did not want to talk; I was tired. But the Holy Spirit prompted me to, so I agreed. First, let's break away from this story for a moment. We need to address something important. I will be brief.

Now, I know some of you are going to raise an eyebrow because you are going to say I used demon spirits to get information. Of course, in the occult world, this practice is called channeling, and mediums allow their bodies to be used by demons to reveal certain information. I am not endorsing that, nor am I suggesting that my experience create some type of doctrine for casting demons out of people. As I stated earlier, this was my first experience confronting demons, and I have learned much more about handling demons since then. However, if you read Mark 5:9, you will find that Jesus asked a demon a question and received information from the demon.

> And he [Jesus] asked him, What is thy name? And he answered, saying, My name is Legion: for we are many.
>
> Mark 5:9

This was not Jesus' common practice—nor is it mine. In recent days, I usually just tell the demon to shut up and come out, just as Jesus usually did. This is why following the prompting of the Holy Spirit is so important. Fundamentalists always want an exact formula, but sometimes God does not operate in the paint-by-numbers approach. You will further notice in this same passage, the demons made a request for Jesus to allow them to enter some nearby pigs, and Jesus allowed it. We cannot make some doctrine out of this, but obviously, God allowed it for that one unique instance. I believe this was the case with Kevin and why the Holy Spirit prompted me to address and talk to this demon and others as part of Kevin's deliverance. That being said, let's continue.

The demon then said, "You know why you are here, right?" I told the spirit that I was there to cast him out. The spirit then said, "No, I mean, you know why YOU are here?" I was puzzled because it sounded like he was being redundant, yet still trying to tell me something. So I said, "Tell me why I am here." The spirit then looked at me and frowned. It said, "Because, you know!" I did not exactly know what it was trying to say, so I commanded it to speak clearly. The spirit then said something that changed my life forever. Reluctantly, it said, "You know about us and our plan. You are chosen!" I knew God was humiliating this demon by forcing it to admit my God-given assignment. Then the Holy Spirit told me to command the demon to reveal its name, and the evil spirit replied, "Hip-hop!" This demon began telling me how it and other demons were deceiving our nation through music, and how music was their primary weapon. At that moment, I understood. I learned more than ever what the devil was doing through music and how the hip-hop movement was going to strike this country with a fatal blow. I was shaken by what this spirit was forced to reveal. Though Kevin's deliverance took three days, eventually because of God's grace and power, Kevin was completely delivered and set free!

Overall, there were forty-two demons cast out of Kevin. And the Lord took us through all forty-two of them, one by one. I know many might say, "All you had to do was cast them all out at once," but the Lord purposed for me to meet and deal with them all for a reason. I learned more about the spirit realm in those three days than in any other time in my life. The last thing any demon wants is to be forced to manifest itself and expose its strategy. God forced these demons to expose Satan's strategy through music. And, yes, since then, I have encountered the spirit of hip-hop in thousands of other people. Think about it: How many other hip-hop artists, like Kevin and Color Me Badd back then, are currently deceived and spreading demonic influence, and need to be set free? Better yet, if the spiritual origin of the hip-hop movement is demonic, does this somehow explain the spiritual and moral decline of our nation's youth, especially African-Americans? Much of this is due to the breakdown of the black family, of course, and the absence of fathers, but the devil has used hip-hop to be a contributor to this plight.

A Generation That Needs Freedom

You see, an entire generation lost its "father," in a sense, when Dr. Martin Luther King Jr. died April 4, 1968. Seeing the influence of the Black church and community on society, the devil knew he had to do something. From that point on, the devil implemented a plan to undermine the Black pastor's impact on culture and the next generation, and replaced the godly influence of spiritually moral leaders with the malevolent influence of his leaders through hip-hop. Back then, it used to be that young Black men wanted to be responsible, strong, and godly men because they looked up to men like Dr. King. In other words, instead of desiring to emulate the character and integrity of pastors and preachers, forty years later, a generation arose that glorifies multiple sex partners, drugs, Thug Life, and prison. Around the time of Dr. King's death in 1968, the elements of hip-hop began to emerge, and a generation searching for its identity left its identity in Christ and went from Christ-centrism, to ethnocentrism through hip-hop. The results have left a run-down people, fatherless still in many ways, in search of identity through sexually immoral lifestyles and false religions. Unfortunately, because this same immoral behavior is running rampant in the church, many Blacks are exiting the church, leaving behind the God who freed us from slavery and abolished segregation laws.

One of the major contributing factors to this problem is the spiritual influence of hip-hop. As you read this book, you will understand that more than a music style, hip-hop is a way of life that is destructive. Like the King Kong example I gave at the beginning of this chapter, we can no longer seek to be entertained by this beast that is beyond our control. Consider these facts:

- 80 percent of African-American children grow up in single-parent homes, most of them fatherless.
- It was reported in 2000, for the first time, there were more Black men in prison (791,000) than in college (603,032).
- Nearly 50 percent of Black teenagers have genital herpes.
- The leading cause of death for Blacks between the ages of twenty-five and forty-four is not heart disease or cancer; it's AIDS.
- Every year since 9/11, almost 50,000 Black Americans join the Muslim religion.

The Bible says that people truly perish for lack of knowledge, and what many people do not understand is that hip-hop is one of the major contributors to these figures.

So, just what is hip-hop? What are the religious and spiritual influences behind it? What other ways is it devastating this generation? Can hip-hop be redeemed, or is it something that needs to be countered? These questions and more will be addressed as you read. Inspired by the DVD series that exposed hip-hop for what it is, "The Truth Behind Hip Hop," is written to equip the church, to expose the enemy's hip-hop strategy of destruction, and to empower you. Together, as we look at the hip-hop subculture in light of God's Word, not only will you be empowered to walk in freedom, but also to set others free. As you read this book, you will understand that hip-hop is more than a music style; hip-hop is a way of life that is leading a generation astray.

In this chapter, you were exposed to the spiritual influence behind hip-hop. In the next chapter, as I finish telling Kevin's story of deliverance, you also will learn more of the principles the Lord has revealed about music's subtle power to transform lives, for good or evil. Together, we will see how music artists are used to further Satan's agenda. But before we do that, let's end this chapter with a simple prayer:

Father God, thank You for leading and guiding me unto all truth. I ask for the spirit of wisdom and revelation, so that I may know the hope of Your calling. I surrender my heart to You and ask You to search it and find any wicked way within me. I want to be free to know Your will and accomplish Your plan for my life. Holy Spirit, strip away the blinders of the enemy so that I may experience the culture of the kingdom of heaven. Empower me to free myself and others from depression, death, sexual sin, and destruction in the hip-hop subculture. In Jesus' name, amen.

Chapter 2

Hip-hop and the Temple of Doom

I remember the last demon that was cast out of Kevin, the former member of the group Color Me Badd. This spirit defiantly sat there and jeered at me through Kevin's eyes, refusing to respond to any words or commands I gave it to leave. I tried everything. Controlling Kevin's face and voice, the demon just sat there, staring at me, and kept saying, "Now, what are you going to do?" I was stumped.

I sat back and prayed, and the Holy Spirit spoke to me and said, "Play some music." I told Kevin's wife to put on a CD I made a while back, with a song on it called "With You on My Side." Kevin always said this song was his testimony. So his wife put the CD on and turned it up loud. I began to watch as the evil spirit's smirk turned into a frown. The demon began to shake and then yelled, "Turn it off!" Of course, I told Kevin's wife to turn up the volume instead! After a minute or so, the spirit covered his ears and yelled, "Noooo!" At that moment, the demon said a few things not worth repeating, and then left! This time, along with the verbal commands to leave in Jesus' name, to cast out this last demon, God used music!

I knew then God was trying to show me how powerful music is, and if it could play a spirit out, then it could play a spirit in! That amazed me, and I learned how the spiritual influence behind music always stays with it. For instance, when I wrote that song, it was my deliverance. So the same power from the Holy Spirit that went into the song stayed with it. And that is what God used to make the final demon leave.

The Lord confirmed this to me with the story of David and Saul. When an evil spirit was tormenting Saul, David played his harp, and the evil spirit left Saul. First Samuel 16:23 says, "And it came to pass, when the *evil spirit* from God was upon Saul, that David took an harp, and played with his hand: so Saul was refreshed, and was well, and the *evil spirit departed from him*" (emphasis added).

That's incredible! David did not even sing, but because of David's close relationship with God, when he played his worship music, God inhabited David's praises, the atmosphere changed, and the evil spirit had to leave. Praise and worship music is a weapon because God inhabits the praises of His people (Psalm 22:3). Unfortunately, so does Satan; he inhabits the praises of his people, too. So just imagine if drugs, sex, violence, murder, and so on are the inspiration for a song. What kind of spirit follows a song created under those influences? And will it chase a spirit away, or will it put a spirit in? These are the questions that we must ask ourselves when we embrace secular music as Christians. Ultimately, music is worship, and whatever you sing about or sing to will come to you. The truth of the matter is this: You summon what you serenade! When you serenade violence, pride, greed, lust, sex, and false gods, you summon dark powers that kill, steal, and destroy generations. Can the devil deceive us into singing about false gods and demonic doctrines? What are the true spiritual origins of hip-hop? How dangerous is the gangsta, Thug Life, hip-hop influence? This is what we will cover in this chapter. To lay a foundation, you must understand influence and the power of our words.

King Solomon said in Proverbs 18:21, "Death and life are in the power of the tongue: and they that love it shall eat the fruit thereof." The English word *power* in this verse is from the Hebrew word *yad*, and it literally means "hand." So it also could say that death and life are in the "hand" of the tongue. The "hand" of the tongue—what does that mean? What it implies is that you can speak a thing, and it is like a hand comes out and creates what you say. God created the whole world with His words, and as co-laborers with Christ, we are to partner with Him by speaking into the natural realm whatever He has decreed from the heavenly, unseen realm. The unseen hand of God begins to shape and fashion what He has decreed for your life when you say things according to His will. Matthew 16:19 says, "Whatever you bind on earth shall have been bound in heaven, and whatever you loose on earth shall have been loosed in heaven" (NASB).

Now, I am not talking about the "Name it, claim it" or "Blab it and grab it" foolishness, where you speak whatever you want (money, cars, and possessions) into existence according to your desire and not God's will, and, Poof! There it is. The kingdom of God does not operate like "I Dream of Jeannie!" The power that Jesus gave you to speak things into existence comes through your relationship and ability to partner with Him. As you can see, what you sow with your words today is what you will reap tomorrow. In other words, what you sow is what you grow.

Now, the Bible says that the devil walks about like a roaring lion, seeking whom he may devour. If he is looking for something he can devour, what exactly is he looking for? Well, he is looking around because he knows he does not have the legal right to use his power on Christians. He may impose his power, but any Christian not in sin can rebuke and resist him, and he must flee (James 4:7). Therefore, he must be cunning in his ability to gain control of you. So if he is walking around looking for some way to exercise power over you, then where is the power? In your tongue!

If you are a Christian, the only authority the devil has is the legal right or authority you give him by what you do in sin and what you say. You can either partner with God or partner with the enemy by your words, whether you realize it or not. Do you realize that everything you have today is something you have said before, from the good to the bad? The right or authority God has given you also has the ability to affect those around you. Therefore, for the sake of those within your sphere of authority, you need to speak life instead of death.

Unfortunately, the unseen hands of demonic spirits also watch over your words. They try to bring about what you say negatively when it agrees with Satan's evil desire for your life. That is why you should never say things to children like, "You aren't gonna ever be anything!" or, "You're gonna be just like your sorry daddy!" because your words have power, and, in essence, the unseen *yad*, or "hand," of your tongue allows demons to take hold, shape, form, and fashion what you say. And yes, this can have a profound affect upon you and those under your influence.

As a matter of fact, *yad* is also translated in the NASB in Daniel 8:25 as "influence." Since *influence* can be defined as "the ability to affect change by tangible or intangible means; consciously or unconsciously," it means there is an unseen realm that tries to influence our visible realm—whether we realize it or not. So it also can be said that death and life are in the "influence" of the tongue. So the question is not, "Am I being influenced?" Rather, the question is, "What is influencing me?" You are probably asking, "Okay, G. Craige, so why is this important to music and hip-hop?"

You see, as a Christian, there are certain things the devil knows you will never say. He knows you will never say that Jesus Christ is not your God. He knows that you will never say that the white man or black man is God (at least some of you). He knows you will never consciously say certain things. He knows he has to trick you into saying it by putting it in music lyrics so that you will sing it! It's important for you to state certain things since the power of your tongue can create or formulate your future. And once you say it, he tries to influence your life. Sound far-fetched? Let's examine how this works.

George Harrison

Now, The Beatles guitarist George Harrison, during the hippie movement, had a song called "My Sweet Lord." Harrison and the other Beatles became followers of the Eastern guru Maharishi Mahesh Yogi, and some embraced Hare Krishna, Eastern religions, and later the occult. Desiring to unite people of different religions together, George Harrison seductively tried to lure in Christians by having them sing, "Hallelujah" in the song "My Sweet Lord." Little did they know, he was just a pawn in Satan's hands to deceptively influence Christians into worshiping the devil.

In the song, he deceptively switches from Hallelujah to Hare Krishna in the middle of the song, deceiving Christians and everyone into saying that Hare Krishna is their sweet "lord." Hold up, is Krishna the same lord that Christians worship? No! According to the Hare Krishna religious book, *The Bhavagad Git*, Krishna is, "I am. . . . He is the lord of destruction, the serpent of eternity, and the prince of demons!" This is what their book describes Krishna as, but biblically, this describes the blasphemous and fallen angel Satan himself!

So why did Harrison do this? Here is what he said about changing from sweet Lord, Hallelujah, to my sweet Lord, Hare Krishna: "My idea in 'My Sweet Lord' was to sneak up on them a bit. The point was to not have people offended by 'Hallelujah,' and by the time it gets to 'Hare Krishna,' they're already hooked and their foot's tapping and they're already singing 'Hallelujah' to kind of lull them into a sense of false security, and suddenly, it turns to 'Hare Krishna,' and they will all be singing that before they know what's happened, and they'll think, *Hey, I thought I wasn't supposed to like Hare Krishna*" (Chant and Be Happy, The Bhaktivedanta Book Trust, 1982, vol. 33).

Satan was deceiving people into worshiping him with their tongue, and seeking to gain their worship and influence their lives. Whether it is false religions or self-worship, Satan ultimately is the false god over them. He will try to draw worship to himself or away from the true and living God by any means. That was back then, with the hippie movement. What about today in hip-hop?

As you now see, when the devil wants to further an anti-God, antichrist agenda, he uses music, and such is the case with hip-hop. Exodus 23:13 says, "And in all things that I have said unto you be circumspect: and make no mention of the name of other gods, neither let it be heard out of thy mouth."

The antichrist is not going to force anyone to worship him, but he wants to "cause" all to do it through subtlety (Daniel 11:12). How will this happen? Well, how do we physically praise and worship a person? In biblical times and throughout history, when the name of a king or important person was said, people lifted their hands as a sign of surrender to their greatness. This is what we do in church when we praise God. One of the Hebrew words for praise is *yadah*, which means to revere or worship with extended hands. Have you noticed that when most secular hip-hop artists are in concert, they make people say their name and raise their hands? They want to be worshiped, especially if they have subscribed to the "self is god" belief system.

One of the most popular rappers of our time is Jay Z. It seems Jay Z believes in the "self as god" concept and has released self-worshiping songs as well. It can be said that Jay Z's songs cause worship of himself as a god. There is one song in particular called "Do You Believe" in which he refers to himself as Hova the god. He calls himself Jay Z, but also J-HOVA. *HOVA* meaning that he is J-HOVA god, as in Jehovah, the god emcee! Also in another song, "H.O.V.A.," he tells people to raise their hands, and most everyone that sang the song and lifted his or her hands did not realize this song is glorifying him! A Sony record executive that worked for Def Jam at the time said after hearing my message, she was stunned when she went to one of Jay Z's concerts, and thousands raised their hands and chanted his name, and did not stop for close to forty-five minutes! Of course, I am not saying that Jay Z is the antichrist, but the antichrist agenda is to deceive and "cause" people to worship a false god. This runs rampant in hip-hop, and many are being deceived and losing their souls behind the worship of false gods through music.

Most people are surprised to learn that hip-hop is more than a music art form and is a way of life. As one of its founders says, "Rap is what you do; hip-hop is what you live." It is a subculture with false religious beliefs from the Universal Zulu Nation, Nation of Islam, Five Percent/Nation of Gods and Earths, Rastafarianism, and other religions, which say that the Black man is god and denies the supremacy of Jesus Christ as the only way to eternal life. To them, Jesus Christ is either one of many gods; is just a prophet, not the Son of God; or is just the white man's God, used to oppress Black people. One of the founders, KRS ONE, whose name is an acronym for Knowledge Reigns Supreme Over Nearly Everyone, says it like this:

"In hip-hop, there are no gods or goddesses. We are the gods and goddesses. We say to each other, "peace god," "peace goddess." This concept has been lent to us from the 5 percent nations of gods and earths. If your religion is Islam, eliminate the distance. Stop worshiping Allah; be Allah. If your religion is Judaism, stop studying the five books of Moses; be the law; be Moses. If you are a Christian, stop worshiping Jesus Christ and calling His name out. Be Christ. Be Buddha. Be Krishna."

Isn't it interesting—when he was talking about not worshiping Allah, just being Allah, that was pretty much all he had to say? But when he got to Jesus, he said for us to stop calling His name out because the devil knows that there is power in the name of Jesus! The devil knows he has to bow at just the mention of Jesus' name! (Philippians 2:10). The devil does not want your tongue to release that heat-seeking missile to his knees!

This belief, that we can be our own gods, is one of the foundational beliefs that established the hip-hop subculture and is taught by KRS ONE in the Temple of Hip-Hop. That is right, hip-hop has its own temple and is recognized as a religion by many. KRS ONE has been instrumental in setting up hip-hop temples across the United States. These temples are set up with elders and doctrine, just like other religious organizations. This will be covered in greater detail when we talk about the origins of hip-hop.

When the founders of hip-hop got started, they used rap as a tool and put their religious beliefs of Black empowerment and false god worship in the lyrics. From hip-hop rappers to hip-hop R&B singers, this practice is still carried out today. Here is just one example from another hip-hop artist.

Erykah Badu

Erykah Badu is one of the most popular hip-hop, "Neo Soul" artists. She first became popular with her hit song called "On and On." Badu is a believer of the Five Percent/Nation of Gods and Earths doctrine, along with many other hip-hop artists. We will explain this in more detail in another chapter. In short, Five Percenters believe that Black people are gods and goddesses. Now, like George Harrison, does Erykah Badu know she cannot make you "say" certain things, and know she has to make you say it by singing it through music? Perhaps.

In the song "On and On," Erykah Badu takes a strange twist when she says that since we were made in God's image, then we should be called our names. What are our names? According to Five Percenters, gods and goddesses. Later, she makes a reference to being born under water with three dollars and six dimes, referring to the 360-degree doctrine of the Five Percenters, which says god is man and woman. Also, her reference to math in this song is referring to the supreme mathematics of the Five Percent doctrine, which says the world was grafted in a mathematical equation.

As you can see, this song is full of her false god worship from the Five Percent/Nation of Gods and Earths! So because she cannot make you confess the devil's Five Percent doctrine, just like with George Harrison, the devil deceptively gets you to worship the Black man as god by singing this song and others. Another artist, Jill Scott, quotes the Quran in her lyrics. That is the so-called positive side of hip-hop; however, what about the negative side of hip-hop and the thug, gangsta hip-hop influence? Beyond the violence, is there more there spiritually than what meets the eye?

In 1984, Steven Spielberg and George Lucas released their second "Indiana Jones" movie, *Indiana Jones and the Temple of Doom*. In it, Jones takes on a secret society of notorious robbers and killers that are enslaving young people in India. Who they are is revealed in one scene, when Jones and his sidekick, Short Round, are hiding in a cave and see hundreds of men bowing before a violent-looking Hindu goddess and chanting. Shocked, Short Round then asks, "What is that?" and Indiana Jones replies, "It's a Thuggee ceremony; they're worshiping Kali." Then, the shaman burns a man alive in a fiery pit, offering him as a living sacrifice to Kali. Later, when they are caught, the Thuggee's shaman, Mola Ram, says, "The Hebrew God will fall, and then the Christian God will be cast down and forgotten. Soon, Kali will rule the world." Of course, at the end of the day, Jones gets the girl, frees the children who are slaves to the Thugs, and saves the day. Though the special effects and stunts were great, as for the storyline, most people I know who have seen this movie were disturbed by its darkness and were glad when they saw "The End."

While everyone clapped at the end and called Spielberg the greatest, the truth is that Kali is real, and the Thugs, in fact, were an underground sect that worshiped this goddess. They were a real group of occult worshippers of the goddess Kali and were considered to be the world's first Mafia-type organized crime society. As a matter of fact, *Thuggee* is where we get the modern word "thug." Though the other Thugs were eliminated in the early 1900s, spiritually, a new generation of "Thugs" are here, and they are enslaving our youth by Satan's influence. Today, hip-hop is the new temple of doom. What do I mean, and why do I say this? Pay attention. Could it be that the same influence is operating through hip-hop today?

Russell Simmons, Kali, and Thugs

Many are familiar with Russell Simmons, who is considered the godfather of hip-hop. He is a multimillionaire and owns many record labels and businesses, such as Def Jam Recordings and Phat Farm clothing. Russell Simmons built a house that was featured on one of the MTV Cribs shows. And in the basement, he has a temple that has the Hindu goddess Kali from India in it. You do your research, and you will learn that Kali is a Hindu yoga goddess of violence, death, and destruction. According to what he said on MTV, he prays and meditates before this statue almost every morning. (Now, you know his momma didn't raise him like that. Seriously, though, pray for him, saints. You will understand why shortly.)

As I mentioned before, Kali had a cult group of followers that worshiped her statue back in the nineteenth century called Thuggees. They were considered one of the first organized gangs, but their covert subculture was spiritual. They were willing to sacrifice money, jewels, possessions, and people to Kali in exchange for her protection and influence. They were robbers and assassins who befriended travelers, then killed them and stole their valuables. Even when people came into the temple and began to worship Kali,

Thuggees killed people by ritualistically strangling them, and stole their possessions.

In our DVD "The Truth Behind Hip Hop Part 3", I show a picture of what these men looked like, and compare it modern day "thug life" rappers. The thugs of old stole possessions and hid them on their bodies. If they had jewelry, they hid it in their mouth, and when they saw another Thuggee, they smiled to show off the jewelry in their mouth, obtained to please Kali. As I mentioned before, later in history, the word "Thuggee" was shortened to the word "Thug," which is the English word we use today to describe gangsters, robbers, and criminals. Russell Simmons worships Kali because of her involvement with the Thugs, and thug life, popularized by Tupac, is now synonymous with the hip-hop subculture. Now, Russell Simmons, who is the godfather of hip-hop, worships before the goddess Kali because she rules over and protects the thugs. Could it be, as a result of Simmons' high-level authority, Kali's influence of death, violence, and destruction is producing a new generation of "Thugs," through Simmons' sphere of influence in hip-hop? Are you listening to me? Do you understand what is happening when you are rapping or singing, "I wanna be a thug, I wanna be a gangsta, I wanna be a criminal?" When these hip-hop artists sing about being a thug, they take on these characteristics, and the *yad*, demonic hands, transform them into the image of a thug. In other words, they become channels for these very spirits because death and life are in the power of the tongue.

For instance, lets take Mike Jones for example. Did Mike Jones look up the Thuggee to see what the Thug looks like before he pursued the music business? A side-by-side comparison of a 19th century thug and a 21st century thug are close to mirror image facial expressions. When you see Mike Jones picture next to a thuggee from old, you see a very accurate similarity! It looks familiar because it is a familiar spirit! Many times when Mike Jones is rapping, he grins so you can see his grill, or jewelry, in his teeth, like a Thuggee from the nineteenth century. Listen! This stuff is older than you think. Slim Thug, Lil Jon, 50 Cent, and Young Buck—these guys are glorifying being a thug. Whether they realize it or not does not matter, most of them are deceived. But as for you, do not be conned. You see, it is still Satan and his kingdom drawing worship unto himself. Ultimately, it is Satan that is recruiting a new generation of thugs to carry out death, violence, and destruction.

Kali has many Hindus in bondage to it, and they need our prayers. Even today, people still make pilgrimages to Calcutta, India, to make sacrificial offerings to Kali. Sometimes those sacrifices are human beings, and sometimes it is their own children. For example, in a *Time* magazine article, it was reported in 2002 that police in Calcutta were arresting people at least once a month for sacrificing humans to Kali! One 23-year-old young lady in the article actually hacked her three-year-old daughter to death because a sorcerer for Kali promised that Kali would grant her money, power, and influence. (Time magazine, "Killing for Mother Kali," July 22, 2002). Of course, that was in India, but what about in America?

Well, who is considered the Elvis of hip-hop? Tupac. He was one of the greatest proponents of Thug Life and Thug Love. Tupac's like Elvis, in a sense, because just like Elvis, he has a group of people who believe he is coming back to life, and they worship him. One of the followers of this cult for Tupac actually beheaded her six-year-old daughter! (June 14, 2005, Seattle Washington, "Seattle Times" and "Religionnewsblog.com" last accessed 5-3-08). I believe demonic Thug spirits of death, violence, and destruction influenced her.

One of Simmons' own Thug Life gangster artists mentioned child sacrifice by glorifying abortion in a song, which spiritually is another form of child sacrifice. Was he under the influence of Simmons' deception to Kali? Perhaps, because he was bound to him by contract, this very well could be the case. In Usher's remix of his song "Confessions," Thug Life rapper Joe Budden makes a guest appearance on one of many versions of this song. This particular version was about Usher cheating and getting the other girl pregnant and being afraid of getting caught. In Budden's rap, he mentions hoping she gets an abortion, and then hitting or shooting her in the stomach if she doesn't. In other words, hit or shoot her in the stomach if she will not have an abortion! This version of the song was on top of Billboard charts until protestors forced radio stations to stop it from being played. However, that same year, there were several reports of men who were arrested for hitting and shooting women in the stomach because the mother refused to have an abortion. Speaking of this, the thug of all thugs, Bone Thugs-n-Harmony, also glorifies abortion in the lyrics of its song "Hell Sent," a grotesquely violent and vulgar song in which they rap about placing grenades inside of women and strangling their babies!

Now, did anybody tell Bone Thugs how the thugs of old ritualistically killed people by strangling them? This is the same spirit, different day, and it is going after the next generation. Incidentally, as of this writing, more than 49 million babies (14 million African-American) have been aborted since 1973 in America, and there are more abortions per capita in the Black community than there are in any other race. Of course, other things are contributing to these facts, but if you do not think hip-hop is influencing this trend, you better think again. Gang activity, Black-on-Black crime, and murder are all glorified in this music. Somebody better wake us up! How long will we continue to allow the *yad*, or hand, of the enemy to influence the destruction of the next generation?

The biblical reality is that scripturally, our bodies are called temples. First Corinthians 6:19 says, "Or do you not know that your **body is a temple** of the **Holy Spirit who is in you**, whom you have from God, and that **you are not your own**?" (emphasis added).

Remember, the good news is that God inhabits the praises of His people, but unfortunately, so does Satan. In other words, you do not have to become a member of the Temple of Hip-Hop or join a gang if you have allowed hip-hop to join itself to you. If that is the case, your body has become the temple of hip-hop, and you are setting yourself up for doom! I know because I have cast it and other evil spirits like it out of people.

When you are under the influence of hip-hop, instead of your mind being a sanctuary for the Lord, it is being infected and filled with degrading thoughts and vile images. Your will is being weakened to do what the enemy wants you to do, and your soul emotionally reacts to the mood of the climate created by hip-hop music. When you serenade violence, pride, greed, lust, sex, and false gods, you summon dark powers that kill, steal, and destroy generations. Do you want your body to be the temple of hip-hop, or the temple of the living God?

In this chapter, you have seen the subtle power of your words, especially through music. What happens when these words are sustained? It creates an atmosphere that can develop into a breeding ground for sin. In the next chapter, we will continue this theme, and you will see how the devil creates strongholds through hip-hop music.

Chapter 3

Atmospheres, Climates, and Strongholds

Young people often ask me, "Can Christians go to secular parties?" "Should Christians go to secular concerts?" "Can we go here or there?" and so on. The real question that must be asked is: What negative effect do concerts, nightclubs, and parties have on you spiritually? In the last chapter, we learned about the power of our words, but when those words are sustained over a period of time, it creates an atmosphere. Atmospheres are created by sustained influence from words that have power. What is the best way to sustain words? Music. Back in the '80s, there was a popular song called *Must Be the Music*, and as you are starting to see, it must be! In this very important chapter, you will see how hip-hop's sustained musical influence creates negative atmospheres, climates, and strongholds in your life.

Before Satan fell, he was Lucifer and was in control of the atmosphere of heaven. Today, this fallen angel is known as the god of this age (2 Corinthians 4:4) and "the prince of the power of the air" (Ephesians 2:2). So, in other words, he is still doing the air/atmosphere thing, right? Also, you know that atmospheres create a feeling. There are some things you desire in certain atmospheres, but you do not feel right doing them in other atmospheres. For example, there are certain things you want to do in the club that you are ashamed to even think about while in church. You see, after an atmosphere has been a certain way for so long, it becomes predictable. Once an atmosphere becomes predictable, it becomes a climate. (All right, pay attention; we are going somewhere!)

Climates are important for natural and spiritual growth. For example, we know that you cannot grow pineapples in certain states like Texas, right? They cannot grow there because the climate is wrong. Since the climate has been a certain way for so long, it has become predictable, to the point that you are conditioned to know what to expect next. It is the same way spiritually, and after an atmosphere stays predictable, it becomes a climate. If atmospheres are about feelings and attitudes, then climates are all about moods. What is the best way to sustain a mood? Music. The word "music" comes from the word "muse," which means to be absorbed in thought; to mediate, ponder, or think upon. Musing upon the Word of God in worship music is one thing, but musing upon the lyrics of sinful, lustful, violent, or demonic music will definitely affect you.

If you stay in them long enough, musical climates will influence you. Music is the only channel of influence that is able to affect both sides of your brain without your permission or consent. (I will explain this research in detail later.) For example, if you go into a building where they are playing a song, talking about "smacking it" and "flipping it" and "shaking it" and "slapping it," eventually, you will want to "smack it" and "flip it" and "shake it" and "slap it"! I mean, for some of us, that happens in the beauty supply shop. All you went in there thinking about was buying hair products. The next thing you know, the beat starts getting to you, and in the background, they are singing, "Ohhhh, Smack it, Smack it!" Before you know it, you find yourself bobbing your head to the beat and do not realize what is happening. You are liable to go up to something or somebody and start smacking!

We have to understand that climates are predictable, and music sets the mood for spiritual climates and conditions your expectations. For example, back in the day, when single guys were trying to have sex on a date, they did not play gospel greats like Mahalia Jackson or The Five Blind Boys of Alabama in their stereo. More than likely, it was one of those begging brothers like Keith Sweat or the Isley Brothers, trying to "get you in the mood" for sexual sin. So now you can understand the climate of the club, and why you see the sleazy dressed people, dancing to the foul, suggestive music with dim lights. So while we are at it, just what's up with the club?

Mesmer and Clubs

Franz Anton Mesmer created the principal concepts within the club or nightclub. It is from his last name that we get the word "mesmerize." Mesmer was an occultist, known as the father of induced hypnosis, and considered a quack by many respected scientists. Nonetheless, he had a strong cultic following of aristocrats in France during the late 1700s and early 1800s. He experimented with anesthetics and wanted to find a different way to hypnotize people and spellbind them. He created what he called a *sanctuary*, but what we call today "the club."

In his sanctuary, Mesmer flashed lights at a certain rhythmic pattern while playing low bass tones with booming beats to manipulate his subject's consciousness. What scientists know today is that this throws off your biorhythms because your heart tries to sync with the external booming beat. As your heart beats at a higher rate, you hyperventilate because you are not properly oxygenated. Once you are not oxygenated properly, to some degree, you begin to lose consciousness and lose your ability to reason.

As a result of Mesmer's study, somebody figured, "If we get them in a room and blast the music loud enough, the rhythm will be hypnotic. We can have anesthetic music. We can make them lose their ability to reason. We will mesmerize them and make people lose consciousness in our sanctuary, the club." Ever wonder how someone can be in a nightclub for four or five hours and not realize it? It is because you lost track of time. You will look at your watch and say, "It's been four hours! Man!" Why is that? It is because the musical climate has mesmerized you.

The flashing lights and the booming bass were all part of a plan to captivate and manipulate you, which is mind control! It's witchcraft! When you are in that climate, and you open yourself spiritually, subliminally or subconsciously (to music lyrics, flashing lights, and booming beats), you are subjecting yourself to spiritual influence, and expose yourself to demonic infestation. You see, there are spiritual consequences to this. Many times, what you do in the natural has spiritual consequences. Do not be fooled. The club was created to steal your consciousness, to steal your ability to reason, and to captivate you.

So at work, you wear your nice suit during the day, or your respectable dress, and at night, it's like you are a different person altogether at the club. Acting like, "Nothing but the dog in me," all up against some stank person. Yuck! You ask folks in the club, "Why are y'all in the club?" The reply sometimes is, "I gotta go, man, I guess. Well, uh, I do not know. Just had to go 'cause it's . . . uh . . . crunk?" They're spellbound and do not realize it.

Now, climates are all about moods, and after you stay in that climate long enough, that expectation becomes an accepted norm, which is a stronghold. In other words, the hold is so strong, you stop fighting and resisting. You quit expecting change and say, "This is the way it has been. This is the way it's always gonna be. This is the way it's gonna stay."

So once you understand the atmosphere, the climate, and the stronghold, you will find out that there are certain things you are doing because the atmosphere is conducive to it. You see, the reason why many people are bound to sin is because they stayed in an atmosphere too long. That atmosphere became a climate, and that climate became a stronghold. When it becomes a stronghold, you have to keep going back to that climate. Remember, certain things grow in certain climates that will not grow in others. Therefore, if the climate is conducive to sin, then you are what 1 John 3 says: If any man practices sin, then the seed of righteousness is not in him. What we are talking about is growth and spiritual seeds from your words. So the question is, What are you growing if you practice sin? Listen, you have to be under a certain atmosphere to grow the seed that is in you.

Now you understand why we go to church and worship God. This is why we go home and create the right atmosphere in our own rooms, in our own homes. (You are doing this, right?) That is why we praise God and we pray to Him. It is why we talk to Him; we are trying to create an atmosphere that nurtures the righteous seed within us. If we do it good enough and long enough, it becomes a climate we can take with us wherever we go because we are manifesting that seed of righteousness. But there is a flip side. See, the righteous seed of God's Word cannot grow in the atmosphere or climate of the club. Better yet, a room, a dormitory, or a house that is made up like the club is not healthy spiritually. Remember, what you sow is what you grow.

Here's an example of this, and the destructive influence of hip-hop music. In Arlington, Texas, in the summer of 2005, there was a block party with many youths. While there, the DJ decided to play the song "Put Yo Hood Up," produced by the gangsta hip-hop/crunk rapper Lil Jon. Some nightclubs, because of the influence it carries, have actually banned this song. The song is basically about representing your neighborhood or gang, etc. In this disgusting and violent song, there is a part where Lil Jon tells people to throw up the sign for their hood, set, or gang, and if they see someone that is a rival, get in their face. In another verse, he tells them to spray the place with bullets, and that is what happened during this song at this party. The word "pandemonium" best describes what happened. "Pan" means "broad range," and "daemon" is the Latin word for "demon." These root words make up the word "pandemonium." Pandemonium ensued, and several fights broke out, resulting in two young men being shot and killed for no reason. As you can see, a large outbreak of demonic activity happened because these youth were under the influence of this song. In other words, spiritual pandemics are real.

Why have artists been deceived into placing their false doctrines and demonic values of death and violence in their music lyrics? Because the demons that influence them know what the Bible says: God inhabits the praises of his people (Psalm 22:3). That means when we praise God, He comes and lives among us. This is what *inhabits* means. This is why we go to church and worship the Most High God and offer praises and adoration to Him: "We give You glory." "We worship You." "We praise You, God." And when we do that, His presence comes and lives. And when His presence comes and lives, the attributes of His presence come and dwell in the atmosphere. After we change the atmosphere by perpetually praising and worshiping Him, it creates a climate. This climate is where healings are found. I am not talking about an emotional feeling because somebody tapped into your emotions. I am talking about a real deliverance change, where you do not go back to what you did before. So, in this climate, we can expect real change to happen. In this climate, the answers to the questions about your life come. That means, your purpose really comes. Your season can really begin. You begin to feel God and hear Him. Know Him and love Him. Things in your life begin to get less important, and He becomes more important. You see, after you dwell in His presence long enough, He gets a strong hold on you by His *yad*, His hand. You give up resisting His will and accept His good plan for your life (see Jeremiah 29:11). God becomes your stronghold (Psalm 59:9), and you rest in His embrace, believing what He says about you. That is when He gets your body and releases His influence through you. This is when you get the power to really do things for Him. Isn't that wonderful? Unfortunately, the demons that control these artists know there is a flip side.

As I travel the country, I hear young people tell me over and over again, "Brother Craige, when I sleep at night, I hear things in my bedroom." They tell me, "I sleep with the light on. I sleep near my mom and dad's room because I hear stuff in my mind." They tell me, "I put certain objects in places, and when I wake up the next day, they have moved somewhere else, and no one else has been in my room." They say, "Sometimes in the night, I know I'm not asleep, and something will climb on my bed and get on top of me. And it will cover my mouth, where I can't speak, and begin to wrestle me. And I begin to try to cry out, but I can't say anything. And I know I'm not asleep, but there is something in my room."

You see, while you're listening to music and artists who believe in false gods, artists who cause you to sing false god doctrine, artists who cause you to repeat death and violence in their lyrics, those words are creating an atmosphere. And after a while, that atmosphere becomes a climate. You can pretty much predict that you are going to do the wrong thing. That means when the phone rings, you will not say no to the person who only wants to use you as his or her sex toy. When those friends come around and want you to do what you said you would never do again, you cannot say no. Then that climate becomes a stronghold, and you give up resisting. You begin to believe the lie "This is just the way it is." You begin to think, *Maybe this is just the way I am*, or, *I was born this way.* Then you try to become a Christian living in sin. You see, the devil inhabits the praises of his people, too. So when the song glorifies another god, the attributes of the enemy come, and the *yad*, or hand, of the enemy controls your life.

Now, what if the stronghold of the enemy is being experienced by thousands of people, millions even, all bound by the same experience as a community? Well, that is when a stronghold that has been sustained becomes a way of life for many, which is a culture. In the next two chapters, we will talk about cultures and subcultures, the demonic origins of hip-hop, and how it is setting our youth up for failure in society. The founding fathers of hip-hop, Afrika Bambaataa, KRS ONE, and others, say that they were visited by a spirit when they founded this subculture. They claim that the spirit was from God, but now I know exactly where that spirit is from. It is from the fallen angel Lucifer, and it has a master plan to destroy values and morals, and distort the way of salvation for our young people. Though we can see how successful the plan has been up till now, with God on our side, we can see the captive set free.

Chapter 4

Hip-hop Subculture: The Beast Within, Part 1

Growing up, I remember hearing the story of a little boy. His father's friend asked them to watch his dog during his vacation because they had a huge, one-acre back yard. The dog's house was set up next to a shade tree in the back yard, and the dog was connected to the tree by a five-foot leash. Whenever the young man approached the dog, it barked viciously, and each day, it came closer to biting the little boy. Whenever this happened, he told his father, and his father would say, "Leave it alone." One day, after another episode of barks and snarling attacks, the dog bit the boy. He ran to his father and said, "Daddy, do something. That dog is bothering me again, and this time he bit me." The father did do something: He spanked his son!

After being disciplined, the son said, "I was not acting mean like that dog, Daddy. You should have spanked that old mean dog, and not me." The father replied, "Son, I told you to leave that dog alone." The son said, "But the dog is in our back yard, and that's where I play." The father then said, "Son, you have the main part of the back yard to play in, and because it is on a leash, tied to a tree, that dog only has a small part of the back yard. It has a five-foot chain and collar that is strong, and it can't break free. That dog can only go so far, but you have to walk past all the freedom you have to play in this back yard to get close enough for that dog to mess with you."

Sometimes, like the boy with the dog, we focus on sin instead of the freedom we have in Christ. This example also illustrates something else. That dog's territory was just a small part within a bigger whole. This story also reminds me of small groups, or subgroups, within larger groups. For instance, cultures and subcultures. Like the angry dog, subcultures, though they may be on a leash or restrained because of the laws of the larger culture, still can have a profound impact, or "bite," on mainstream society. Like the angry dog, the closer you get to negative subcultures, the more harmful they become, and such is the case with the subculture of hip-hop. In this chapter, we will discuss cultures and subcultures.

Hip-hop is more than a music genre; it is a way of life, which describes a culture. However, the kind of culture that it is is a subculture, and there is a huge difference between the two. In these chapters, you will see how hip-hop is destroying the spiritual lives of many as they seek to be entertained by music from a subculture beyond their control. What is hip-hop? Is it the same as rap? How are its demonic roots destroying society today? You will understand this and more as you read the next two chapters. First, to get a better understanding, let us take a look at cultures and subcultures.

Webster's defines a culture as "the integrated pattern of human knowledge, belief, and behavior that depends upon the capacity for learning and transmitting knowledge to succeeding generations." The word "culture" comes from the word "cultivate," which is a farming term. When you understand how they work, this makes sense. Cultures are cultivated like soil, by the ideas, religious beliefs, values, education, and principles when they start. The influence of these roots will determine the way of life, which is the cultivated fruit. Since cultures are subject to movements of people based on situations or circumstances they surround, it means that every culture has a base. And the base, or root, decides the fruit the culture will have. As you will see, when it comes to cultures, the roots determine the fruit! The same goes for subcultures.

A subculture is defined as "an ethnic, regional, economic, or social group exhibiting characteristic patterns of behavior sufficient to distinguish it from others within an embracing culture or society." As a subgroup within mainstream culture, subcultures (especially negative ones, like hip-hop) are self-absorbed and talk about themselves constantly. Their feelings of rejection cause most to be "anti-the establishment" movements that tear down or deconstruct the main culture. Subcultures usually empower the low self-esteem of their insecure members by promoting rebellion. Subcultures are distinct because of the desire of their members for uniqueness and self-expression extremely different from the main culture.

As a result, subcultures attract followers who feel rejected by society, who are searching for identity, acceptance, and affirmation. Some even support horrible extremes. For example, attempting to make sense of their emotional pain, kids in depressing subcultures, such as emo and goth, cut themselves and have extreme piercing as forms of self-expression. Knowing this helps us understand why most negative subcultures are birthed, because of some lack or deficit in a person's life, especially a father's validation.

Now, those within the subculture symbolize their connection to it based on their music, fashion, styles, mannerisms, colors, hand signs, graffiti, slang, lingo, and so on, which outsiders will not initially understand. Subcultures must have their behavior regulated and legislated by the main culture, whether it's street gangs who steal and vandalize, or skateboarders who skate where they are not supposed to, or drug traffickers or hate groups, such as the KKK.

"Wannabes" and "Street Cred"

The alluring fruit of a negative subculture is its rebellious mystique of bad boy/naughty girl images that feed the alter ego of mainstream pleasure seekers. So, it is easy to see why subcultures have sales and marketing appeal. People and marketing firms from mainstream culture will adopt fashion and music from subcultures to get "cool" points, look "hip," or somehow obtain "street credibility."

Many of these are intrigued "wannabes" and "posers" that are unaware of the root ideas and beliefs that create the subculture's music and styles, such as the root religious and spiritual meanings of Rastafarian dreadlocks and Polynesian tattoos. (We will discuss this in a later chapter. People in the dominant culture use the music and images from subcultures to escape reality or be entertained.

The leaders of subcultures are the only ones that make any income that affords them an opportunity to progress in the main culture. The followers within the subculture, because their style of dress, attitudes, and mannerisms differ so greatly from mainstream culture, struggle with getting legal paying jobs and being accepted by society, which reinforces their ideas of rebellion, rejection, and victimization.

For example, Satanist rocker Marilyn Manson may make money as the leader of goth, wear makeup, dress and act lewd, and so on, but goth followers that embrace who he is and what he stands for will not fit mainstream society. Many, instead of changing, would rather blame society for their state in life. That is why followers struggle with excelling in the parent culture unless they transform the way they think and change the way they act, dress, and so on. Remember, in subcultures, leaders profit at the expense of the followers being set up for failure.

So the devil knows if he wants to indoctrinate a people with corruption, all he has to do is raise up a music superstar in a subculture because a fan is a true follower. Did you know that? *Fan* is short for *fanatic*, which means the same as *crazy*. Now, you will not find this in Webster's, but one definition of a fan could be "a true follower that's crazy enough to emulate and defend the foolishness of his or her leader." Have you ever noticed how some people go to great lengths to defend their favorite recording artist, regardless of what he or she does? They will say compromising things like, "Well, you pray for him, but man, his beats are just slamming." Some people will defend folks like R. Kelly to the core. "You do not need to judge. You can't judge him." Yes, I can. To judge means to discern, and at the least, we can discern that something's out of whack with R. Kelly. Some folks will protect and defend him because a fan is a follower. Some folks are even worse with Michael Jackson. They do not even know him, and call him by his first name, as if he's their buddy. "Michael wouldn't do that." Michael Jackson has successfully changed his own image into that of a female, and yet his fans still say, "He's not like that. He wouldn't do that to that child; he wouldn't," like they just got off the phone with him! "Naw, he wouldn't do that, not Michael. I watched him grow up."

The fans begin to follow after the artist's or leader's rebellious lifestyle, mannerisms, language, and conduct because a fan is a follower, and followers are worshipers. Imitation is the highest form of worship. For example, when Grunge rock star Kurt Cobain committed suicide, many of his true fans followed after him and committed suicide shortly after he died. This is why the Bible says, "Do not be conformed to this world" (Romans 12:2). To conform means to change from the outside by pressure, and you must resist the outside pressure from the world to look like it or emulate sinful worldly people to be accepted.

Followers in subcultures do not make it or function in mainstream society, and Satan plans it that way. What they do not realize is that they are supporting a dark, invisible subculture that tries to negatively influence cultures in the natural realm.

Spiritual Cultures and Subcultures

In the spirit realm, the subculture is the kingdom of darkness, run by its rebel leader, Satan. Because of man's fall, all the world systems lie in the power of the evil one (1 John 5:19), as he is the god of this age, the spirit that works in the sons of disobedience (Ephesians 2:2). Therefore, he controls much of the world systems affecting politics, economies, and cultures in the natural. Because man is still a free will agent, he is still open to God's influence, his own desires, and resisting Satan's agenda. Therefore, Satan uses subcultures to create intense, passionate followers who start movements to bring rapid change in nations. Most people are deceived and just caught up; however, a few know exactly who they are working for. For example, this is what happened with the hippie subculture. It became the sexual revolution and led us to aborting babies in less than twenty years! Unbeknownst to their followers, many hippie rock groups of the era, such as The Rolling Stones and The Beatles, were in the occult.

You see, Satan, through his one-third subgroup of unseen fallen angels or demons, seeks to take humans into hell with him and hinder the Lord's plan of salvation. He seeks to tear down or deconstruct any natural culture that embraces the values of the kingdom of heaven by his human agents. As the leader, Satan is the only benefactor of his subculture. He benefits today at the expense of his followers' eternal damnation tomorrow, but inevitably, he will spend eternity in hell as well (Revelation 20:10).

The good news is that in the spirit realm, the dominant culture is the kingdom of heaven, run by Jesus Christ. The Lord through His unseen angels and visible human agents, seeks to influence visible laws and governments in cultures within nations. He does this to provide the opportunity for people to get saved, receive eternal life, and further the values of His kingdom. This invisible kingdom is represented in the natural by the church. By definition, because it is characterized as a systematic opposition to the kingdoms of this world as heaven's representative, it is a counterculture.

Many hip-hoppers think they are saved because they have created an earthly, cultural Jesus instead of receiving the true Jesus from the kingdom of heaven. When hip-hoppers get music awards, isn't it strange when they say they are saved, and, "To God be the glory" and, "Thank You, Jesus" for degrading songs? Why do they think they are saved while still embracing sinful lifestyles? Hip-hop has made Jesus fit its subcultural likes and dislikes. It has "buffet Christianity," having picked over what it will and will not accept from the Bible, thus fashioning another Christ in its own image. It is a "Well, I can't help it" false Christ, who forgives when they do wrong, but neither wants or expects them to change their detrimental direction in life. You must understand, when Jesus first came to earth, He did not come to be a resident. He came here as a visitor from another residency, heaven, to invite us to change our residency to His kingdom, which has a counterculture not of this world (John 18:36). What do I mean?

Yes, Jesus came to subcultures in His day, from Herodian political zealots and shady tax collectors to religious Pharisees and sex industry prostitutes, but He only visited; he did not change addresses, set up residency, make every facet of the subculture His way of life, and absorb its values. When He was in the world, He was not of it, and knew that assimilation would compromise His influence. He was a man of conviction, not compromise. He adapted in situations, but never adopted the world's ways. He visited earthly subcultures and lived before them the freedom He enjoys in His way of life, from heaven's counterculture.

Yes, today He still comes to our earthly cultures and subcultures to invite us into in His kingdom. But anything from our culture, from its values and behaviors, that conflicts with His kingdom must go before we enter His kingdom. He will not conform to the ways of our culture; we must repent and be transformed by the ways of His kingdom!

Repentance is not an emotional response from a person who cries about his sin, yet never stops it. A pain of mind is one thing, but a change of mind is another! Repentance comes after forgiveness. Repentance is when the person who is crying because he understands how what he did was wrong has changed his thinking. As a result, he pursues a different direction. Therefore, as for hip-hop, everything from hair, fashion, and lifestyles connected to worship of another god, as well as false religions and belief systems, inappropriate, vulgar speech, immorality, and mannerisms that do not line up with or represent His kingdom culture must go. We must repent, change our mind, change our ways, and submit to the values and behaviors in His counterculture: the kingdom of heaven. For His kingdom to come, our kingdom must go.

When Christ comes the second time, He will not be a visitor. There will be a new heaven and new earth, and Christ will reign forever (Revelation 21:1). He will set up residency here on earth, and the cultures on this earth and every kingdom on earth will be given over to Him. Inevitably, the knowledge of His glory will cover the earth "as the waters cover the sea" (Habakkuk 2:14), and the kingdoms of this world will become the kingdoms of our Lord and Christ (Revelation 11:15). On that day, the culture of heaven will be the only culture on earth. Until His return, however, it is Christ's will that none should perish, and that society benefit from the righteous values, justice, and morals in His kingdom. In anticipation of that day, Christ followers are to proclaim the Good News of His victory on the cross, set captives free, and influence society. This is our Great Commission (Mark 16:15).

As you can see, negative subcultures are run by Satan's rebel human agents and demons. These leaders and their followers are deceived by Satan into rebelling against the reign of the kingdom of heaven, and are being set up for failure in this life and the afterlife. How does this relate to hip-hop as a subculture?

The Leper Subculture

Luke 5:12-15 says, "And it happened when He was in a certain city, that behold, a man who was full of leprosy saw Jesus; and he fell on his face and implored Him, saying, "Lord, if You are willing, You can make me clean." Then He put out His hand and touched him, saying, "I am willing; be cleansed." Immediately the leprosy left him. And He charged him to tell no one, "But go and show yourself to the priest, and make an offering for your cleansing, as a testimony to them, just as Moses commanded." However, the report went around concerning Him all the more; and great multitudes came together to hear, and to be healed by Him of their infirmities."

This is an amazing story. There is more to this story than a man being healed of leprosy; rather, this is a story of a person from a subculture being healed and restored to society. In this time period, leprosy was a problem disease. Because some lepers could not feel pain in their limbs, they had to watch being too close to open flames because they could not feel fire. They could not feel pain, and many times lepers were covered in wounds. Everywhere they went, they had to shout, "Unclean! Unclean!" The reason they did this was to make sure no one else caught the disease. Anyone who came within five feet of the leper was considered unclean and had to endure a meticulous cleansing process in order to be allowed into the temple to worship. When people saw lepers coming, they ran in the opposite direction. Can you imagine how rejected and humiliating it was to say, "Unclean" over and over again? At first, it was about their medical condition, but over time, "unclean" became part of their identity. As a result, lepers were not allowed into the temple and lived together with other lepers in leper colonies. For the Jews, the temple was the center of social life and mainstream culture, and the leper wasn't part of it. The leper colony was their subculture of people who felt rejected by society.

When this leper saw Jesus, he said, "If you are willing, I can be clean." And Jesus replied, "I am willing; be cleansed." The word "willing" in this verse really conveys God's heart toward this person, bound to this subculture of lepers. The Lord could have used a word for "willing" that means to make a decision based on a set of options before you. The other word for "willing" means "unforced and voluntary, of one's own accord." This is the word for "willing" that our Lord used. In other words, He said, "I want to heal you; I don't have to think about it. I want to heal you now." Jesus prayed for the man, and the leprosy left! He was completely healed! Jesus didn't want him just to be healed, however; he wanted him restored to the place where he could function in society. How did he accomplish this?

Jesus then told the ex-leper, "Don't say anything to anybody, and go to the priest, and let him declare you healed." Why did he do this? The only way the ex-leper was to be restored back into temple life and Jewish society was if he was declared clean by the priest. If the leper told anyone that he was cleansed by Jesus, because they hated Jesus so much, the priest would not have declared him clean. Because he followed the Lord's instructions, not only was this ex-leper delivered from leprosy; he was restored back into temple worship. Because he followed the Lord's instructions, the leper was restored to mainstream culture and able to function in society. Family and friends who were not allowed to touch him could embrace him for the first time, and years of rejection was broken. No longer unclean, his cleansed soul was free to worship God and tell of His marvelous works. He was set free from the subculture of lepers in a leper colony and became an ex-leper who showed God's transforming power to the world.

God wants to do the same thing for people bound by today's leper colony: the subculture of hip-hop. Like the leper, many are bound by hopelessness and rejection. Many are numb to the pain of life because they have seen and experienced too much, too soon. They think they've been burned and wounded by life so much that they cannot feel anymore. Because of the way they look and dress, society calls them thugs, gangstas, and unclean. When people see them coming, they go in the opposite direction. They are a subculture of fatherless rejects, longing for truth and a loving embrace. To them, Jesus doesn't say, "Let Me think about healing you." No, He says, "I am willing. I want to heal you. I don't have to think about this; I want to heal you now." Their transformation will be so powerful, they will not look like thugs, gangstas, and unclean people any longer. God will heal them of their wounds and make them productive in mainstream society for the benefit of His kingdom. Because they've been changed from the inside, the outside will change as well. Instead of curse words, they will speak blessed words. They will not sag or wear grills or get tattoos because they know they are now part of God's kingdom, and as royal family members, anything carnal or negative is beneath them. And when other lepers from the colony of hip-hop see the hope in their eyes and their love for life and God, they will ask, "What must I do to get what you have?" And the ex-hip-hopper can introduce them to Jesus. It's interesting that though this leper was told not to say a word, this story went far and wide, and according to the Bible, everyone heard about this. God wanted this man to become a sermon that everyone could see. I've heard it said, "Preach the gospel at all times; if necessary, use words" (St. Francis of Assisi). Once you are no longer unclean, everyone will know. Just like the leper, you must follow the Lord's direction, and you will be changed to spread His Good News. It's time to get out of the leper colony of the hip-hop subculture and become a saved kingdom representative in Christ's counterculture.

Chapter 5

Hip-hop Subculture: The Beast Within, Part 2

Now that we have laid a foundation, let's get into the nuts and bolts of this. Remember, the spiritual roots and origins of any subculture are key to understanding its influence upon others, and such is the case with hip-hop. In other words, hip-hop is a subculture, and the music is its fruit. As KRS ONE says, "Rap is what you do; hip-hop is what you live." Hip-hop was used to describe a way of living, not just music. There are television commercials that used to run on BET and MTV that state, "Hip-hop is not music; it's a way of life," and, "You do not *do* hip-hop; you *are* hip-hop!" This clearly tells us what the agenda of true hip-hoppers is. It's a manifestation of a belief system that governs the behavior of its followers. How did it get started?

During the seventies, just before the movie *Roots* came out, African-Americans were renewed to a greater sense of identity and purpose, and a spiritual shift took place once this movie came out. A part of this self-discovery was positive. African-Americans gained a healthy respect for our slave ancestry, and we learned that many of the slaves were kings and queens. We also reconnected to the great contributions the continent of Africa gave to the world. Somewhere along the way, however, some of us went from Christ-centrism to ethnocentrism, even in many churches. As a result, the hip-hop subculture was birthed out of a desire to manifest one's self in a society that was deemed unfair to African-Americans in the seventies.

It was during this time that New York gang leader Afrika Bambaataa turned his bad gang into a "good" gang. Because of the negative environments and social situations that plagued the Blacks at the time, Afrika Bambaataa and others created a way of temporarily overcoming these social obstacles by partying, making music, and believing in one's self and one's own power. They began holding block parties for neighborhoods, spoke about Black empowerment, and spoke against Black-on-Black crime and gang violence. These parties were called hip-hop parties, and they were viewed at the time as an opportunity to preach a newfound doctrine of self-worship and hate for the establishment.

Somewhere during this period of his spiritual quest for knowledge, Afrika Bambaataa learned about the Ama-Zulus, and embraced the Zulus philosophy and religious beliefs regarding the Black man being god. Eager to share this information with African-American youths, he met with rappers and disc jockeys KRS ONE, Grandmaster Flash, and Kool Herc. KRS ONE, in sharing his account of this on MTV years ago, said he and others were visited at different times and overwhelmed by a spirit that revealed itself to them as hip-hop. From this, they say they were given the strategy on how to advance the knowledge of self as an avenue of empowerment across the country to African-American youths. They chose music as the vehicle of transferring this knowledge of self, using rap initially.

Hip-hop targeted rap music and created music to preach a message that empowered the Black race as "true gods" and made Jesus Christ and the Bible the "white man's religion." This is why hip-hop rapper Chuck D from Public Enemy said in the rap "Bring the Noise," that he thinks Farrakhan's a prophet that he thinks we should listen to. Farrakhan is the leader of the racist cult The Nation of Islam, which refers to Jesus as a mere prophet and the white man's God.

As a result of Afrika Bambaataa's understanding and deception, he believed regarding the Black man being god, he formed The Universal Zulu Nation, and he fused other beliefs that supported his views to shape the hip-hop subculture. Some of you may remember

Bambaataa's song "Planet Rock." Back in the day, it was one of the most popular beats ever. Well, if you remember, at the beginning of the song, he mentions the Zulu Nation, yet, at that time, nobody was thinking about it, but what he was talking about was The Universal Zulu Nation.

The Universal Zulu Nation and Five Percenters

Here is what Afrika Bambaataa's Zulu Creed says: "We believe in one God, who is called by many names, Allah, Jehovah, Ra, Elohim, Jah, God the most high . . ." Hold up! Ra? Allah? They are not the names of the God of the Bible. It goes on to say: "We believe in the holy Bible and the glorious Quran and all the Scriptures of the prophets of God." Hold up! The Quran? Now the Quran is the book that says Allah had no sons. And if Allah is supposed to be god, and Allah had no sons, then what about Jesus, whom the Bible claims is God's only begotten Son? (John 3:16). That is why Allah is not the same god as the Christians' God! They also say, "We believe the Bible has been tampered with and must be reinterpreted." This is false doctrine. The Bible is the inspired, infallible Word of God (2 Timothy 3:16).

Later, Bambaataa found similar beliefs that supported his beliefs, and he now says that he is a god. As a result, the major spiritual influences of hip-hop come from The Nation of Islam (whose leaders have said that god is a Black man and white people are blue-eyed devils), its splinter group The Five Percent/Nation of Gods and Earths, Rastafarianism, components of Christianity, and other religious beliefs meshed together. The problem with all this, of course, is that if Jesus is not Lord of all, He is not Lord at all, and naming Jesus as one of many other false gods denies His claims of supremacy. Jesus said that He is the resurrection and the life (John 11:25). He also said, "I am the way, the truth and the life, no one comes to the Father except through Me" (John 14:6). Hip-hop believes that God has many names—Jesus, Allah, Buddha, Jehovah, and so on. Hip-hop holds the Quran in equal regard with the Bible, which they believe is tainted and full of errors and not the infallible Word of God.

What is a Five Percenter? Five Percenters are an offshoot of The Nation of Islam and are called Five Percenters because they believe that 85 percent of people are blind to the truth about the world in which they live. They believe 10 percent of people understand much of the truth, but use it to their advantage to keep the 85 percent under their control through religion, politics, entertainment, economics, and other methods. The Five Percent are those Black people they consider enlightened divine beings, or gods, because they have repossessed the knowledge of the truth regarding the foundations of life and oneself, and seek to liberate the 85 percent through education. They believe the Black man is god and the Black woman is mother earth. Clarence 13X, a former Nation of Islam leader-turned-self-god-teacher, founded the Five Percenters. He believed he was equal to Allah and therefore left The Nation of Islam to start his own belief system. They believe that Jesus Christ is the white man's deception and way of influencing the Black men of the world into worshiping a white god.

This sick doctrine sounds crazy to a true believer of the Bible, but do not be fooled. This is what many of our Black entertainers believe, and to them, their fame is proof that they are like gods or should be revered as gods. It is in their music, in their interviews, and in their behavior! They are self-serving and high-minded, and they hide these teachings and doctrinal beliefs in their music. Hip-hop artists such as The Wu-Tang Clan, Rakim, Poor Righteous Teachers, A Tribe Called Quest, Brand Nubian, Busta Rhymes, Alicia Keys, Lauryn Hill, Jill Scott, Maxwell, Erykah Badu, DeAngelo, Wyclef Jean, The Roots, and Common are just a few of the hip-hop artists that espouse these beliefs in one form or another, many of them putting this doctrine in their music lyrics. Some, like India Arie, believe in ancestral worship and spiritism.

How seriously have these roots been recognized? On December 17, 2002, the New York State legislature actually issued a resolution acknowledging Afrika Bambaataa and The Universal Zulu Nation as the major founding influence in the hip-hop subculture. The subculture of hip-hop, with its religious and philosophical ideology shaped by KRS ONE and Afrika Bambaataa, is also recognized by the United Nations. The 2006 Hip-Hop Awards also acknowledged this, with many artists bowing before Afrika Bambaataa dressed in his ceremonial attire as a Zulu god with headdress and scepter in hand, which brings us to another point.

Hip-hop has established several worship centers called The Temple of Hip-Hop, started by KRS ONE. KRS ONE is its prophet, they have their own elders, and they teach the hip-hop doctrine. The following is growing nationwide, and more temples are being established. The New York Temple of Hip-Hop reportedly has about a thousand members. The previously mentioned artists feel that hip-hop gangster rappers are giving hip-hop a bad name and feel the previously mentioned artists are providing a safer and positive alternative. Unfortunately, they are deceived and do not realize that hip-hop is leading them and many away from Jesus Christ, the true and living God, the only eternal answer for salvation. This is why I say that saying holy hip-hop is like saying holy Buddha because hip-hop is recognized as a religion. Hip-hop is more than the four elements of rapping, MC'ing, breakdancing, and graffiti. The fifth element is hip-hop's knowledge base, which holds all the other elements together, and much of that knowledge base is the religious influence of false religions that say that Jesus Christ is the white man's God.

Hip-hop taught the youth at the time, and still teaches indirectly, that you can be who you want to be, in the sense of not being what people want you to be. There is a certain truth to this, but if taken the wrong way, it turns into rebellion against basic laws and truths that govern our society as a whole. Hip-hop began to change the very appearance of its followers by creating a look, a way of self-government, and its own unique language. What this created was a subculture within our American culture, and it caused our youths to go against the basic pattern of society and manifest their own will, regardless of what it cost them socially and spiritually. I guess there is truth to the saying "If all you see is what you see, then you will believe that is all there is." If you can grasp these next statements, you will understand why hip-hop has been so successful in the "hood."

By growing up in impoverished neighborhoods and ghettos, many of our Black youth began to believe that their role models needed to be found among their peers. They saw pimps making all kinds of money, so they emulated the pimp by dressing like him, talking like him, and pretending to be him. They saw thugs and gangsters going in and out of prison, so they began to walk like them, dress like them, and emulate them. Hip-hop was birthed out of poverty and in the streets of New York, where the "in" thing at that time was selling drugs, pimping, and going in and out of prison.

So our young boys began to emulate the look of thugs and gangsters because there were no real positive role models among them to emulate. Our young girls began dressing like the loose women they saw on a day-to-day basis. Furthermore, whatever they had to do out of lack became the "style." For instance, white tees and jeans became the style because that is all some could afford. Dickies work outfits became stylish because they were cheap and affordable. Hip-hop became a way to get the Black man notoriety and show that the lower-income Black people of America had a voice. In and of themselves, there was nothing wrong with some of these fads. However, some of them led to embracing hopelessness.

Inadvertently, what Bambaataa and his entourage did was glorify the street life and make being in the streets, and of the streets, acceptable. Over time, the wrong things were celebrated and empowered by a new group of leaders. Sure, Bambaataa, KRS ONE, and others taught self-respect and self-worth, but they did it from the wrong level. Instead of pulling the youth of this nation "up," they made those that were "down" the mark to shoot for. In other words, they reinforced the idea that society is unfair to the Black man, and in many cases, it still is. As a result of this over emphasis, feeling victimized in a society they learned to hate and distrust through this subculture, and believing they could not succeed in society through normal avenues, the hip-hop follower had to turn to another measure of success. Therefore, a new group of leaders emerged in hip-hop, and instead of pointing the youth to the work force, the business world, higher education, or entrepreneurship, as it evolved hip-hop eventually made thugs, gangsters, hoochies, and pimps its representatives.

Hip-Hop Gangstas and The Dark Side

While other artists lend themselves to the more spiritual/mystical side of hip-hop and have been deceived by the enemy, hip-hop is also the destructive spirit behind the violence, hatred of women, and gang activity we see in groups like 50 Cent, Eminem, Snoop Dogg, Ludacris, DMX, and a host of others. Most of the performers within hip-hop glorify greed, self, materialism, sexual promiscuity, and everything else contrary to the will of God. Much was said in 2007 of the Don Imus controversy; he was the radio shock jock who was fired for calling the Rutgers women basketball team "nappy-headed hos." What he said was definitely racist, sexist, horrible, and wrong. The hip-hop industry, however, has been saying this for years! If Don Imus gets fired, then we must also fire degrading hip-hop artists like Snoop Dogg, Ludacris, and more, and the record companies who distribute their filth, like Sony and Arista!

Hip-hop seems only to care about living out its creed, which can be summed up in the title of 50 Cent's movie, *Get Rich or Die Tryin'*. Hip-hop has moved from false god worship and idolatry into straight-up blasphemy as well. One rapper mentioned earlier, Jay Z, not only has gone so far as to call himself Jehovah as his nickname, but he actually has a back-mastered message on one of his songs, "Lucifer" (the DJ Danger Mouse remixed version), where he or someone says "666, murder, murder, murder, Jesus . . . 666."

Hip-hop is also growing more and more dark with groups like Three 6 Mafia (that's right, this group's name is the mark of the beast, 666), whose lyrics are blasphemous and demonic. Lord Infamous of the group raps often about drug abuse, murder, and Satanism. Strangely enough, these performers claim to be Christians! Many hip-hoppers, from them to DMX, claim to be Christians, extending their following into the church. They thank Jesus in their award shows, or even connect with well-known Black gospel artists and pastors, and continue to spew sex, violence, and death in their other lyrics. What fellowship does light have with darkness? None. Rappers who are truly Christian would not sing about or emulate anything contrary to God's will. While people can be redeemed, subcultures must be countered, and hip-hop, like every worldly subculture, must be countered by the influence of the kingdom of God.

Now, hip-hop has literally changed the face of our nation. It has caused our youth to lower their standards and set their sights on themselves and their own feelings, rather than taking the harder road to success. They now see what is acceptable or fashionable to our society as being "weak" or "wack." Hip-hop has turned our young boys into thugs and our young girls into young whores. It has caused marijuana and other illegal substances to become acceptable among our youth, and it is stopping our people from achieving real success. The followers of hip-hop are set up for failure in mainstream society, while the leaders profit at their expense.

Whether we want to admit it or not, we must adhere to the fact that we live in a society that promotes educated, properly dressed, well-mannered men and women. Hip-hop, however, tells our youth that it's okay to wear your clothes like a criminal or dress like a bum. It's okay to look evil and talk in slang as long as you stay true to the subculture of hip-hop. But the scary part is many want the church to accept hip-hop as a way to reach the youth who are currently involved in it. I believe this is a big mistake, and here's why.

Redeeming Subcultures or Redeeming People?

Personally, I see nothing wrong with Christian rap as an entertainment device, as long as Christian rappers do not emulate the spiritual or negative aspects of the hip-hop subculture, and stay away from saying or invoking hip-hop in their lyrics. Rap is a tool; it is a method of communication. But hip-hop is a spiritual influence, belief system, and subculture. Paul said he became all things to all men in order to win some (1 Corinthians 9:22). He did this by creating communication bridges, and he used those bridges to pull people out of darkness, instead of using the bridges as a vehicle for him to cross over and fully assimilate into the worldly culture or system. In Acts 17:22-34, Paul's Mars Hill example truly reveals how to be in the world, but not of it (John 17:16). We are also commanded not to love the world or the things in the world (1 John 2:15). Also, we are not to be conformed to the world, but rather we are to be transformed by the renewing of our minds (Romans 12:2). So the question is, "Can hip-hop be redeemed?"

Listen, God does not take subcultures and make them holy; He takes people. He takes prostitutes every day and saves them, sets them free, and makes them holy! He takes drug addicts and crack addicts every day, saves them, and makes them holy. Those who belong to the red-light subculture, the goth subculture, the drug subculture, the hippie subculture, the gay/lesbian subculture, and the streetwalking subculture are saved, set free, and delivered, never returning to the way of life from which they were delivered. But when He makes them holy, are they still what they once were? Are the prostitutes "holy hos"? Are the drug addicts "holy crackheads"? Are Hindus "holy Hindus"? Or are they new creations? They will be new creations that will not resemble their old ways, and are ex-pimps, ex-gangsters, and ex-hip-hoppers. Once they have been transformed by the renewing of their mind, they no longer think, act, or desire to look like that from which they were delivered. It is called repentance (see Acts 3:19)! Once God has changed our minds, we change our ways and turn in the opposite direction. Gospel gangstas, preachin' pimps, and holy hip-hoppers are not new creations, but they are spiritual mutations that retain portions of who they were, and thus are flawed. They are not new, but just amended. They are not hot, but lukewarm, a mixture of hot and cold. This is exactly what God said He will spew out of His mouth—those who desire the world and God (Revelation 3:16).

The roots of the hip-hop subculture are demonic and are similar to other subcultures with an anti-establishment, "down with the man" mentality. Fatherlessness, rebellion, oppression, anguish, poverty, violence, and other negative influences created this subculture. Zulu customs, Black Muslim teachings, and other false religions established the so-called "positive" aspects of hip-hop. Thugs, gangs, drugs, sexual promiscuity, and prison life make up the other overtly dark facets of hip-hop. You must realize that God did not play a part in the creation, establishing, or foundation of hip-hop, so how can we drag Him into it at this late stage? When KRS ONE and Afrika Bambaataa say they were visited by a spirit and the spirit influenced them to accept their callings into hip-hop, how can we embrace this subculture when its origins are evil, demonic, and destructive to society?

Even though all music has a strong element of influence, hip-hop has an entire subculture. Remember, the music is the fruit of the subculture's influence. This demonic influence is affecting the Black community as well as white American youth, as more than 70 percent of this music is purchased by white youth. If another "wangsta" or "wanna-be Black" white kid rolls up next to my car at a red light and starts bassing his hip-hop music, bouncing his head to the beat, while throwing up a peace sign at me, looking for approval, I think I'll throw up! Since Black nationalism is so ingrained in hip-hop, the very artist these kids are listening to may very well hate them! In the Latino community, with its version of hip-hop, la raza, with its MS-13 gang influence, it is plain to see that the devil is an equal opportunity employer.

This music and its demonic influence have affected our youth and young adults in a way that no other tool of the enemy could have. The devil has deceived them. How else can you get young people to be proud of ignorance? How else can you make the decline of morality a trend among our youth? How else could you make a nation of young and old people accept drug users, murderers, rapists, Satanists, and people who defile our children's morality as a trend and applaud it like an art form? How else could you cause young people to act out pornographic sexual acts with no boundaries? How else can you glamorize degrading things like getting arrested, going to jail, having multiple sex partners, conceiving kids out of wedlock, smoking weed, murdering, committing crimes, and doing other things once considered vile by anyone's standards? The influence of hip-hop music is destroying our youth.

Though the Temple of Hip-Hop was established in 1996, the founders of hip-hop began influencing hip-hop music and subculture long before this place of worship was finally established, allowing us now to see it for what it is. It is a demonic belief system that is pondered and mused upon every day in the music our youths are listening to, with an ideology full of self-exaltation and false god worship. Beyond this, other gangster hip-hop performers are promoting greed, sexual promiscuity, and murder.

I mentioned this before, but I must say it again. The biblical reality is that scripturally, our bodies are called temples (1 Corinthians

6:19). You do not have to go to New York to become a member of the Temple of Hip-Hop, or join a gang, if you have allowed hip-hop to join itself to you. If that is the case, your body has become the temple of hip-hop! This is not a "play thing" in the spirit!

When you are under the influence of hip-hop, instead of your mind being a sanctuary for the Lord, it is being infected and filled with degrading thoughts and vile images. Remember, when you serenade violence, pride, greed, lust, sex, and false gods, you summon dark powers that kill, steal, and destroy generations. Are you going to be God's temple, or hip-hop and the devil's temple, and be deceived by materialism and sexual sin and become another statistic?

In ABC News' "Out of Control: AIDS in Black America," they report a CDC study on AIDS. In it, they reveal that 50 percent of all new AIDS cases nationwide in 2005 came from approximately 13 percent of the population, African-Americans! Also, that same 13 percent, African-Americans, account for more than 37 percent of all abortions nationwide. AIDS and abortion are many times the consequences of sexual immorality. Its no wonder many believe the Black race is decreasing. Musing on sexual immorality, death, and idolatry is killing us off. As I said before, hip-hop is a temple of doom, and its worship music is a death march.

At one of the hip-hop summits, it was touted that hip-hop has created twenty-six millionaires. The leaders of the summit said this should be celebrated. The question that should have been asked is, "At whose expense?" You see, these artists are promoted by the devil, and they are rewarded with riches to keep the people who listen and follow them impoverished. The followers of hip-hop are not going to make decent livings or get well-paying jobs, nor will they fit into society by dressing like thugs, sagging their pants, or wearing grills in their mouths! I mean, do you really think "naw mean?" or "for sheezy" will go over well in a job interview? As a matter of fact, "sagging," doo rags, Dickies, and braids were adopted by hip-hop from prison subculture. Because mainstream culture does not embrace hip-hop attire as a whole, the followers are set up for rejection and the one place their attire is embraced, which is hell on earth—prison!

You see, hip-hop's leaders may get gun charges, even murder charges, but their high-powered attorneys manage to get them off. Worse yet, now Satan has improved his strategy. Why not arrange for them to be arrested and get community service with a few weeks or months in jail, all timed when a new album drops? As the CD sales "blow up" as the hip-hop leader leaves court, the followers can "high-five 'em" on their way in. Only problem is the followers' outcome is prison, and their stay is much longer! The hypocritical leaders of hip-hop spend more time behind bars on the set of a video than they do in reality. Three to Five minutes on a video is not the same as three to five years in a real prison! You see, those who continue acting like they deserve to go to prison eventually wind up going there. Could it be that the twenty-six millionaires of hip-hop are responsible for the thousands of Black people caught up in this subculture that are now in prison? Perhaps, because whatever leaders do in moderation, the followers will do in excess. For example, Black men, who make up just 6 percent of the population, account for more than 40 percent of the prison population. Also, consider these stats:

- In 1980, Black men accounted for 143,000 men in prison, and 463,700 were enrolled in college.
- In 2000, Black men accounted for 791,600 men in prison, and 603,032 were in college.

As you can see, during the twenty-year period that hip-hop gangsta rap was on the rise, more Black men went to prison than to college! Many of those men join The Nation of Islam and other Black Nationalist organizations for protection while incarcerated. Because the music influence of hip-hop was Black Nationalist idealism ingrained in false religious beliefs, is it any wonder that these men have been led into literal prison and spiritual prison? And they are not the only ones. As mentioned in the first chapter, since 9/11, every year, 50,000 Blacks convert to the Muslim religion, and of that number, 80 percent were former Christians.

But then again, what about when you are pleasure seeking (which many times is really sin seeking) and buy hip-hop as a way of entertainment and escape? I am sorry, but those "cool points" cost too much; your quest for "street credibility" is supporting somebody's disability; you are a "poser," en route to becoming a loser, and your attempt to be "hip" is funding the hype! You see, you may not start doing drive-bys or become a Five Percenter, but someone younger and more impressionable will. For the sake of amusement, you are bankrolling the devil's agenda of destruction by seeking to be entertained by a beast you cannot control.

In the next chapter, you will see the progression of how God led me to understand the goth subculture and its connection to Satan's hip-hop agenda for our youth.

Chapter 6

What Kind of Music Is That? (The Vision)

It was in 1990 that, while in prayer, the Holy Spirit began to show me a vision, and the revelation from it began to shape my life. During this encounter, the Lord said to me, "There is some music out there you need to know about; it's called heavy metal. The devil is trying to show himself to the white youth of America through heavy metal." The vision and God's words lasted only a moment, but more revelation came to me as I began to ponder this. More clearly than ever, I could see what was happening. Around the same time that I had this revelation in 1990, ABC News aired a "20/20" documentary about the dangers of heavy metal music and how the white youth were killing each other and etching things like "666" in their chests. They were worshiping false gods and reading the Satanic Bible. At the time, there were rock groups sacrificing animals to the devil on stage, making the concert attendees drink human urine, and all kinds of other filthy acts of rebellion, in worship of Satan.

Groups like Black Sabbath, whose very name is synonymous with a day Satanists offer human sacrifices to Satan, produced songs that celebrated evil and were lyrically ungodly. Ozzy Osbourne, who was the lead singer for Black Sabbath, sang about the devil and glorified everything that was evil. He even bit live bats' heads off on stage at his performances and led his audience into worship chants to Satan. Groups like KISS (which people referred to as <u>K</u>nights <u>i</u>n <u>S</u>atan's <u>S</u>ervice), W.A.S.P. (<u>W</u>e <u>A</u>re <u>S</u>atan's <u>P</u>eople), AC/DC (<u>A</u>nti<u>c</u>hrist <u>D</u>evil <u>C</u>hild), Megadeth, and others were leading our nation's youth into rebellion with their on-stage antics and their lyrical content.

Many of their songs promoted death, suicide, murder, sex, and drugs, and their followers many times indulged in these acts while under the influence of these rock stars. This music was spinning out of control, and many youth were spinning right along with it, and suffering because of it. Even in rock and heavy metal concerts, deaths and injuries abounded. This is because the audience became so excited about their celebration of the underworld, they physically slammed into one another and broke each other's bones in response to the atmosphere of violence and darkness that these artists created through their music.

During this time, parents and teachers were alarmed as children that were drawn to this subculture began to radically change. The kids became rebellious and disrespectful, influenced by the lyrics and practices of their rock stars, and our nation's leaders became concerned. Music had always influenced our nation's youth, but now we had a form of music that was violent and perverse, yet popular among young listeners. The music did not just play into them, but it began to change them. They began to alter their appearance to resemble the darkness within the music. The goth look became popular among teenagers, and they began to resemble dead people and look like the walking dead in their schools and neighborhoods. I can remember seeing kids as early as the fifth grade wearing KISS shirts and carrying lunchboxes of hard-core heavy metal artists. Not only did the kids start looking like their rock heroes, but they also started behaving like them. We started seeing suicides that could later be traced to lyrics that spoke of ending your life. We began to see murders that could be traced back to lyrics that encouraged death and killing. Even though our nation wanted to ignore the effects of music on our youth, no one could honestly deny that many of the problems were being influenced by the music of our nation's rock star performers.

I guess the scariest part of this subculture was its satanic undertone. Rock stars were not just promoting violence, death, drugs, and sex, but they were straight up worshiping Satan and promoting his kingdom! They had "666" on their album covers or many times written on their bodies. You could see all kinds of satanic symbols and Antichrist sayings on their album covers and in their lyrics. For example, the upside-down crucifix to mock the death of Jesus; the five-point pentagram, which symbolized witchcraft; the head of Baphomet, the half man/half woman goat that is worshiped in Satanism and the occult; and many other symbols were popular on the clothing of the youth and the album covers of these death metal bands. It was as if the floodgates were open, and heavy metal music and devil worship went hand in hand. Many satanic symbols were popularized by many of these performers and used to promote the kingdom of Satan.

The Satanic Bible became popular at this time by Sir Anton LaVey, the founder of the church of Satan. It was used by many rock artists and promoted by this subculture because it denounced God and Jesus. Because of the rebellion of this subculture, many kids that wanted attention subscribed to it. This subculture promoted things that were opposite the norm so that you could be individualized and gain attention by going against that which was deemed normal. This was rebellion at its peak, and all the things considered good and right were denounced by this subculture. Life was replaced by death, good was replaced by evil, human waste was celebrated as something good, and obedience was replaced with rebellion. God was replaced with the devil, and worship was replaced with selfishness. Many church youth groups began to suffer as this rebellious culture of kids denounced God and the church. Groups like Megadeth, were singing about being the devil's advocate and being his salesman in songs such as "The Conjuring."

Heavy metal was on the rise, and the subculture of kids that followed it were suffering in their everyday lives. School grades dropped, the morality of the students declined, and their desire to succeed in this life began to drop off. The devil had something he could negatively influence our nation's youth with, which was protected by the Constitution of the United States under freedom of speech. Our nation was suffering, and many were praying for a change.

The Holy Spirit further revealed to me that the devil was not satisfied with the popularity of heavy metal music because the majority of youths of all races were not buying heavy metal music. Heavy metal never had enough mass appeal to influence many other races beyond white, suburban youth. Notice that the music of heavy metal was not the draw. The sound of it is not appealing to the ear. So what was it that drew the youth? It was the rebellious nature. Because it went against traditional music and the artists dressed bold and different, heavy metal had appeal. Traditional values and attire were mocked and shunned by these performers, and as a result, the kids started to rebel against what was considered the norm or appropriate. Even though our society had guidelines for dress and appearance in the workplace, in schools, and in certain establishments, the death metal bands promoted what was against these guidelines and forced their followers to rebel and go their own way. At the same time, this subculture stopped its followers' progress in the real world, which caused people to judge them based on their appearance, rather than who they really were.

You see, even though our youths want to be expressive in their attire and behavior, we must realize that there are social norms in a nation, and conforming to those norms is essential for progress in that nation's society, or national cultural norm. I am not advocating total conformity and uniformity of a dominant culture. However, I am saying that teaching youths to maintain their individuality at the expense of not fitting into places of employment, schools, and other establishments to further their life's purpose is a grave mistake. The subculture that is formed by these musical artists usually digresses from the norm, and it many times keeps our kids from excelling in conservative venues, where attire and behaviors are regulated. Therefore, once our youth reach the age of employment, they must learn workplace ethics and know how to fit into society without attempting to make a statement about themselves through their subcultural expressions. This rebellion became very popular among the goth subculture that followed death metal and heavy metal music in the 1980s.

The artists were in direct defiance of our society's rules of proper dress and basic morality, and this became very appealing to youth who wanted to rebel against the norm and get attention. Goth was the subculture, and heavy metal was the music.

Goth Subculture

As they began to negatively influence suburban white youth of America, it created a twofold dynamic. It caused youth to rebel in ways that enslaved them to the artists and at the same time caused them to be rejected by society. After all, the artists could prosper in the subculture because they were the leaders of it. Therefore, they could dress weird, act crazy, and do all the things that their way of life promoted and still maintain a level of income and business sense without conforming to the rules of our society. Yet, the kids that followed them were ridiculed, outcast, and shunned by society as a whole because they became too extreme in their expression. As a result, they were looked over for jobs and also made to feel inadequate. In addition, the more people shunned their behavior, the worse their behavior became because they were feeding off the negativity and rejection they were receiving. They wanted attention, and they wanted to stand out, so they became more and more extreme in their rebellious expression while all along displacing themselves from their purpose in life and following a lie that ultimately blocked their ability to excel.

Parents told their kids to behave a certain way, and these artists behaved just the opposite. And remember, what the leader does in moderation, their followers will do in excess. Consequently, rebellion portrayed by goth leaders was attractive to young fans, and they took what their music artists portrayed to higher level. Goth followers began stirring up controversy and going against the norm in their homes, schools, and everyday lives. And the more people tried to stop them, the more they felt they were being rejected, abused, or outcasts. They saw the rejection of their actions as people imposing their standards or religious rules on them. But what society or the main culture was rightfully regulating was their extreme expression. As a result, while the artists prospered, the followers were rejected, and this led to many suicides, murders, and sacrificial deaths because these kids were outsiders and did not fit the societal norm. But because the music was not very attractive to the masses and because our country was still, for the most part, governed by the acceptance of moral values, heavy metal music was not appealing enough to expand its reach to youth of all races on a mass level.

There was still a greater audience for the devil to influence, and heavy metal was not going to do it. God continued to show me that Satan had plans to unleash a subculture of music birthed from the African-American community, but it would cross all cultural boundaries. He also showed me that this subculture would infiltrate the church as well. What God was revealing to me is the music we know today as hip-hop, but it is not a music form; it's a lifestyle, a subculture, influenced by religions whose purpose is to totally replace God with a false belief system.

I found this very difficult to accept at first because as I knew it, Black folks were not "down" with the devil. I know that statement may sound stereotypical, but in the circles where I grew up, we as a people did not embrace Satan as a deity that we worshiped. We may have indirectly served him, but we as the Black race, as I understood, never directly offered praise and worship to Satan. We respected God and the church more than we respected ourselves, for that matter. We could be in sin, getting "krunked up in da' club," but if someone in the club yelled, "SATAN," we would immediately fall to our knees repenting and crying out to God! It was like, we were sinners, but we did not want to be down with the devil! I know that is warped, but there was a certain respect I grew up with, and most people in my day believed the same way. I even remember listening to ungodly music, but turning it off when we drove past a church. (I admit that it was a hypocritical respect for God, but it was at least a level of respect.) We did not claim the devil, Satan, or evil, for that matter. Although we were in sin, we always believed that God was God and that the devil was not to be toyed with. Worshiping Satan and denouncing God, as a Black person, was unheard of in my day.

Until this time, rap music had been pretty innocent. Rappers generally rapped about their sneakers, gold chains, girlfriends, and musical ability, and singers usually sang about going out, hanging out, and spending their paychecks. The motive was to make music that people could dance to. Many of the early hip-hoppers did not make much money on their records; they were just happy that people liked their music.

The worst group during the early era of rap music was probably 2 Live Crew. Now, this group was greatly used by Satan to prevent obscenity laws from stopping crude lyrics in rap music. It was also the first group to popularize hedonism and lewd sexual behavior in rap music. I even had the opportunity to speak with Bro. Marquess, who penned songs for the group, including "Me So Horny." He informed me that the group actually paved the way for perversion in music to be openly accepted by listeners with no legal intervention from censors. However, the group was not directly or openly worshiping the devil. The group's music was devilish, but not occult, but soon, hip hop artists began moving further into the kingdom of darkness.

Chapter 7

The Vehicle of Rap

I can remember when God began to show me how rap music was going to take a turn for the worse and become the vehicle for the antichrist to use to cause our youth to accept false religions and immoral values. He began to tell me, just as the heavy metal subculture of goth was destroying the lives of America's suburbia youth, hip-hop was going to do the same, but with greater numbers because of the greater music appeal. I remember one day being at my parents' house and flipping through the television's cable channels. I was sitting in my parents' home, and they had a video service called "The Box." This video service allowed you to order a music video anytime. So as I was watching music videos, a video came on by The Almighty RSO, aka "Made Men." As I was watching this video, which looked like a regular rap video, I could not believe my eyes! One of the rappers turned around to reveal "666" shaved on his head!

I had seen this type of stuff in heavy metal music, but to see it on the head of a rapper was shocking to me. Now, I can remember old soul and R&B artists that were sexually explicit, but never had I seen them openly promote the mark of the beast (Revelation 19:20)! Even when we were in sin, we never played with that number. That was the number most of us had never written in our lives! We avoided it like the plague! I remember times when I was in the grocery store, and my groceries rang up $6.66, and I would purposely get some gum or a *TV Guide*, just to change the number! That was the number you did not want on anything, including a printed receipt. So to see these guys use this number as a promotion of evil was shocking, and I could tell that the devil was up to something. The Holy Spirit reminded me of what He told me regarding music and hip-hop. He said, "Here it comes." Hip-hop artists began to do collaborations with Satanist rock groups. For example, DMX did a song with Marilyn Manson, an avowed church of Satan priest! *The New York Times* also noticed this trend, and reported, on September 18, 1994:

"Public Enemy sampled the Satanist band Slayer, Ice-T collaborated with them on the soundtrack for the horror film *Judgment Night*, and Cypress Hill put a Gothic-looking graveyard on the cover of its latest album, *Black Sunday*.

Not until this year, however, have hip-hop bands been willing to complete their move from the streets to the graveyards. "I'm the resurrector," the Gravediggaz rap on their first album, *6 Feet Deep*. "Be my sacrifice. Commit suicide, and I'll bring you back to life." For those who cross the Gravediggaz, a band made up of members of the Wu-Tang Clan, Too Poetic, De La Soul, and Stetsasonic, death is only the beginning of their punishment. "First I'll assassinate 'em," they rap on "Diary of a Madman." "And then I cremate 'em, and take all of his . . . ashes and evaporate 'em."

I became so alarmed that I printed up fliers explaining what God had showed me about the "new music" that was coming to lead the Black youth of America into worshiping Satan, and how the church also would embrace the music. My music group went around to churches and neighborhoods to sing and pass out brochures, and people laughed and jeered at us. Many people tore the fliers up in our faces and said, "This will never happen." But unfortunately, it has! Ten years later, we saw the unfortunate results of the music.

Around this time, a few days later, I was watching "The Box" again, and I saw a video called "Nuthin' but a 'G' Thang" with Snoop Doggy Dogg and Dr. Dre. The sound was unlike anything that anyone had ever heard. This music was like "ear candy," the beat was "bumpin," and the lyrics were "tight." The Holy Spirit spoke immediately and said, "That's it! Gangsta rap. This is the vehicle the devil is going to use." I did not understand that statement because they were not doing anything that I thought was devilish. Snoop was on Dre's 1992 debut *The Chronic* as much as Dre himself. Thanks to the singles "Nuthin' but a 'G' Thang," "Dre Day," and "Let Me Ride," *The Chronic* was a multi-platinum, top 10 smash, and the entire world of hip-hop changed with it. For the next four years, it was virtually impossible to hear mainstream hip-hop that was not affected in some way by Dr. Dre and his patented G-Funk. Not only did he produce Snoop Dogg's 1993 debut *Doggystyle*, but he orchestrated several soundtracks, including "Above the Rim" and "Murder Was the Case" (both 1994), which functioned as samplers for his new artists and production techniques. "Murder Was the Case" actually went triple-platinum! The weirdest thing about this CD was that it made it to the pop charts! Yes, that's right, the POP charts, which at the time were dominated by mainstream American music. I even remember the top three songs on the Billboard pop charts were:

1. The theme from *Forrest Gump*,
2. The theme from *The Lion King*, and
3. "Nuthin' but a 'G' Thang!"

This was crazy because the song glorified the ghetto, the streets, thugs, gangs, and weed smokers. These were all the things that our nation considered unacceptable, and yet, because the music was so good, it surpassed the intellect and understanding of the record companies and made them rich! I knew then that if it kept selling at a rapid pace, there would be no restrictions placed on the music. As a result, it would be free to fulfill the evil purpose that the enemy had for it.

I remember seeing another video on "The Box," but this one took a more demonic turn than the previous Dre and Snoop collaborations. The video was *Murder Was the Case*, Snoop Dogg's debut solo album. The song depicts the story of how Snoop Dogg was gunned down in Long Beach, California, where he lived. While he lay dead, he was visited by Satan. He states in the song that Satan made him an offer to bring him back to life and make him rich and famous. But there was a condition to this deal, which is the very theme of this story. Satan asked for Snoop's soul in return for life and riches. He told him that he would have "eternal life forever" and would give him everything he ever wanted, as long as he promised his soul to him. The CD even came with a DVD movie depicting events in Snoop Dogg's life and even talked about his death and resurrection.

Murder Was The Case

This story rapped about in *Murder Was the Case* is true, according to Snoop, and is also true among many industry singers and performers. Many of them confess to exchanging fame and fortune for damnation in the afterlife. It's not an uncommon thing because most of them promote sex, sin, violence, and lust anyway, so eternal damnation is almost warranted by our modern-day performers and glory-seekers.

In this same video, *Murder Was the Case,* there was also a very disturbing scene of Snoop Dogg smoking weed in his car. As he lights the joint, the vapors manifest into Satan, and when he inhales, Satan enters his body through the smoke of the marijuana! This was a bold statement to make, but most of these gangsta rap artists will tell you they need marijuana to create their music because it sets the mood. I have personally been told by a well-known ex-hip-hop gangsta rapper that when they walked into the recording studio, they could not function unless they first smoked weed and got high! But what they fail to realize is that marijuana is a hallucinogen, and when you smoke it, you open yourself up for demonic infestation. As a result, the enemy is able to use your body and mind with very little resistance from your will.

Many creative artists use this drug and others help them relax and become more creative. The Bible calls this sorcery (Revelation 21:8; 22:15). The English word "sorcery" is the Greek word *pharmakia.* Within this word, it is easy to notice our modern English word "pharmacy." *Pharmakia* is also translated as "drugs" as well. In Bible times, shamans and sorcerers would give potions to drink, chew, or smoke for money. Usually, the drugs were made of natural herbs and other ingredients. When ingested, it opened the buyer up to the spirit world for demonic influence and inspiration. That was back then, but what about drug users today? Unfortunately, it is the same spirit, different day. As a matter of fact, modern-day crystal meth and speed manufacturers call themselves "wizards"! As for people who use drugs for inspiration, what is really happening? They are being used as a host for the devil. He is gaining control of them to get his purpose accomplished through their creativity. As I said before, they become the temple of doom.

Of course, most drug dealers and buyers are ignorant of the spiritual connection and do not realize that biblically, they are sorcerers, on their way to hell if they do not repent. Revelation 21:8 says, "But the cowardly, unbelieving, abominable, murderers, sexually immoral, **sorcerers**, idolaters, and all liars, shall have their part in the lake which burns with fire and brimstone, which is the second death" (emphasis added).

There is another shocking scene in this video, where Snoop Dogg is lying dead in a room, and a crow flies through an open window of the same room. The crow lands on a chair and turns into Satan. Satan then approaches Snoop and passes his hand over his eyes as if to put a spell on him. After that, Satan stands and turns into Jesus Christ, a Jesus with thorns on his head and nail impressions in his hands. Then he turns back into Satan! This was shocking to me because I had never seen biblical blasphemy like this in any rap video before. This was blasphemy, just as Jesus described it in the Bible when He addressed those who claimed He did works with Satan. Jesus said that if you say His works are the works of the devil, then you blaspheme, and it is unpardonable! Mark 3:22-29 says,

"And the scribes which came down from Jerusalem said, He hath Beelzebub, and by the prince of the devils casteth he out devils. And he called them unto him, and said unto them in parables, How can Satan cast out Satan? And if a kingdom be divided against itself, that kingdom cannot stand. And if a house be divided against itself, that house cannot stand. And if Satan rise up against himself, and be divided, he cannot stand, but hath an end. No man can enter into a strong man's house, and spoil his goods, except he will first bind the strong man; and then he will spoil his house. Verily I say unto you, All sins shall be forgiven unto the sons of men, and blasphemies wherewith soever they shall blaspheme: But he that shall blaspheme against the Holy Ghost hath never forgiveness, but is in danger of eternal damnation."

In this video, Jesus was depicted as the devil, and the devil was depicted as Jesus. What a shocking sight this was to me. Later I learned that in the occult, Luciferian world, they believe that Jesus and Satan are equals and were brothers. Of course, the truth is that Jesus Christ has no equal, and Jesus Christ is God's only begotten Son (John 3:16). Satan's closest equals in the kingdom of heaven are God's angels such as Michael or Gabriel. This video is portraying Luciferian doctrine. It really made me pay close attention to what I was viewing and listening to from that point on.

Everything the Holy Spirit had spoken became clear to me about a week later. At this time, I saw a video with the group Bones Thugs-n-Harmony. Now, Dre and Snoop sounded good, but this music was the most alluring music that I had ever heard. I am a musician and producer by trade, but I had never heard anything that sounded this good to my flesh. I felt like my soul was being pulled into the television. I immediately sensed a spiritual/soulish element to the group's music. While I was enjoying this, the Holy Spirit quickly arrested me; He said, "Watch out!" I was later introduced to the lyrics by some youths at my church. Bone Thugs proved to be some of the most influential rappers of this era. They mix satanic flows with mesmerizing vocals and chants. And they have mixed plenty of Christian-oriented lyrics in their music as well.

They have enclosed in their first CD a "Mr. Ouija," which is a paragraph written backwards. I researched this and found out that in ancient Salem, the witches sent letters to people written backwards. A person would have to look into a mirror to read it. Well, I began to read the "Mr. Ouija" in the mirror, and the Holy Spirit said, "Stop!" I asked why, and I heard the Lord say, "The reason the witches wrote notes backwards is because when you read it in the mirror, you are actually speaking a curse directly into your soul!" Luke 11:34-36 (NASB) says:

"The eye is the lamp of your body; when your eye is clear, your whole body also is full of light; but when it is bad, your body also is full of darkness. Then watch out that the light in you is not darkness. If therefore your whole body is full of light, with no dark part in it, it will be wholly illumined, as when the lamp illumines you with its rays."

You see, your eyes are the window to your soul. By reading "Mr. Ouija" in the mirror to my own reflection, I was actually cursing myself. Can you imagine how many young people have done the same thing? It must be understood that this CD sold more than 10 million copies.

I remember there was a fifteen-year-old boy who heard me speaking this message, and he told me that he read this "Mr. Ouija" during a church service! He said that he read and decoded it when he was twelve years old. Then he said that it took effect on him immediately and that night, he started a three-year ritual of molesting his baby sister. His deliverance came that night when he heard the truth about it, but only after three years of regretful, shameful acts of perversion. How sad! Can you believe that a rap group as occult as this could sell that many records to hip-hop and R&B lovers? This sounds like Ozzy Osbourne or Alice Cooper, not a mainstream rap group. This was, however, just the beginning.

Bone Thugs also perform witchcraft-type practices in their videos and photos, such as levitation, crystal ball readings, Ouija board activities, séances, and plenty of weed smoking and praying. In one of their videos, they even mock the cloven tongues of fire that appeared upon the disciples' heads in the New Testament, while gathered around a crystal ball. They are definitely down with the devil.

One time I was speaking this message at a church, and a fifteen-year old boy told me he was deeply into Bone Thugs. He brought me a sawed-off twelve-gauge shotgun. He said, "Please take my gun; I do not know how many people have been shot by it." He also told me, "Preacher, I've learned a man cannot just kill another human being; your conscience won't let you do that. So what we do is something we call "ride or die." What we did was listen to Bone Thugs-n-Harmony continually until we lost consciousness. At that point, I could kill my own mother."

I knew after this, there was no return for this new type of music. It was here to stay. This music became universally accepted by all races and began to top the Billboard pop charts. God began to show me the future effects of this music. He showed me how young people were going to start glorifying things that are evil, such as going to prison, sagging their pants, filling their mouths with gold; our girls would dress like prostitutes and still be accepted. Do you know that one of the greatest role models among young people today is a thug? Only through music could the devil make right seem wrong and wrong seem right.

Chapter 8

The Devil in Heaven

After all this, I was very alarmed. I was like, "God, what is going on?" I knew Satan was behind it all, but God began to tell me that in order for me to understand what was happening, I had to learn more about Satan and his true abilities. I knew he was the devil and was on his way to hell, but what I did not know is that his origin was heaven. You see, when God created Satan, he was not Satan as we now know him, but he was Lucifer—the son of the morning. Bible scholars believe that as the worship leader of heaven, he was created to be the first sound heard in the morning.

He was made to usher in the presence of Jehovah God. He was beautifully built, and his being contained the most precious stones imaginable. With the beauty of the stones, he also had creative sound-producing elements. He had viols or pipes in his body and percussive instruments like the timbrel for rhythm. Before there was ever a "human beatbox," God made Lucifer, the angelic "beatbox"! He was uniquely made and was a very special being. Look at how the prophet Ezekiel visualized him:

Thou hast been in Eden the garden of God; every precious stone was thy covering, the sardius, topaz, and the diamond, the beryl, the onyx, and the jasper, the sapphire, the emerald, and the carbuncle, and gold: the workmanship of thy tabrets and of thy pipes was prepared in thee in the day that thou wast created.

Ezekiel 28:13 KJV

Isaiah 14:11-12 (KJV) states:

Thy pomp is brought down to the grave, and the noise of thy viols: the worm is spread under thee, and the worms cover thee. How art thou fallen from heaven, O Lucifer, son of the morning! how art thou cut down to the ground, which didst weaken the nations!

The word "viols" in this verse is the Hebrew word *nebel*. In the King James Version of the Bible, it is translated as "viol" (a string, violin-type of instrument) and also as "harp" in the New American Standard Bible. Strong's Concordance also says it means "psaltery," which was an ancient string instrument played by plucking its chords, much like our modern day guitar.

Many of us confuse who Lucifer was with what Satan and demons are now. Now, there are various demons assigned to invoke different feelings and attitudes, such as the demon of lust, the demon of drug addiction, and so on. These are demons, or evil spirits, but Lucifer was created with one purpose, and that was to worship God. He was an instrument, and he could make sounds that changed the very atmosphere. Lucifer prepared listeners' ears and hearts for the entrance of the King of glory. However, because of the influence he had and his ability to manipulate with music, he got beside himself and felt that he should be like God and rule his own domain. This is what he said:

"I will ascend into heaven, I will exalt my throne above the stars of God: I will sit also upon the mount of the congregation, in the sides of the north: I will ascend above the heights of the clouds; I will be like the most High."

Isaiah 14:13-14 KJV

It is interesting that Lucifer, the fallen angel, says in this verse that he would sit above, or rule over, God's other stars. Biblically, stars represent angels and influence.

Stars and Influence

There is something about influence that few people realize. The original definition of "influence" is mind-blowing. In 1918, according to Webster's, the original definition of "influence" was "an ethereal fluid, which flows from the stars, that changes the behaviors of humans." (Isn't that a trip? Stay with me; we are going somewhere important.)

It turns out that "influence" and "influenza" are related words. Any flu, or viral epidemic, was believed to be something that originated from the stars, and carried out the stars' desires to make the masses sick. It once was believed that any person who had widespread fame or epidemic popularity was said to have favor with the stars, or influence. As a matter of fact, the second definition in the 1918 edition of Webster's says that "influence" is "an occult power that derives from the stars." Those involved in astrology, horoscopes, witchcraft, and other occult practices seek their influence from the stars. This is why God said in Deuteronomy 4:19 says, "And beware not to lift up your eyes to heaven and see the sun and the moon and the stars,_all the host of heaven, and be drawn away and worship them and serve them."

You see, the natural stars we see are symbolic of another group of unseen stars: angels. Today, influence basically means the seen or unseen power to persuade or bring about change, and God's angels and Satan's demons carry supernatural influence to effect change in the natural, which brings us to my point. Remember, in Isaiah 14:13, Lucifer said that he would exalt himself above the stars of God, which were God's angels. Because of his pride, he was cast down, and when he fell, he became a fallen star, or fallen angel, and the other angels he influenced fell with him as well. Revelation 12:3-4 says, "And another sign appeared in heaven: behold, a great, fiery red dragon having seven heads and ten horns, and seven diadems on his heads. *His tail drew a third of the stars of heaven and threw them to the earth* (emphasis added).

So God kicked him out of heaven, and a third of the bad stars, or fallen angels, that were persuaded by him fell to earth as well. His name and nature was then changed from the heavenly being Lucifer to the fallen deceiver Satan. The nature of the stars, or angels, that fell with him were changed as well. He was cast down to the earth, where he could rule demons and humans that choose the ways of his kingdom.

As you have seen, stars are biblically symbolic of angels, good or bad, but stars also represent God's people. God's people are also to be like stars and are called to release godly influence. Abraham's offspring of faith, all Christians, are stars (Genesis 15:5). Also, Philippians 2:15 says that as Christians, we are to shine like stars in the midst of this crooked and perverse world. Daniel 12:3 says, "Those who have insight will shine brightly like the brightness of the expanse of heaven, and those who lead the many to righteousness, like the stars forever and ever" (NASB).

We are to be like the star that led the wise men to Christ, and lead people to Him (Matthew 2:9). God's people are His stars that release His influence because we are in relationship with the Bright Morning Star, Jesus Christ (Revelation 22:16). God wants us to have influence, but He wants us to use it the right way and lead people, not unto ourselves, but to Him.

Unfortunately, this means that people who do have epidemic popularity and fame, but are using influence to promote Satan's values of sin, sex, perversion, death, and darkness, are not stars, in the biblical sense. They are leading people away from God and into Satan's hell. They are just mere celebrities, whose favor comes from Satan, the fallen star, and their influence, like the flu, is making a whole generation sick! Satan, the counterfeiter, once again has copied the star concept from God. Even Satan's occult symbol, the pentagram, is a star. In the entertainment world, "star" is the symbol or term that describes a rock "star" and movie "stars." Most are just mere celebrities who promote Satan's agenda.

There is a biblical difference between God's stars and Satan's celebrities. While true stars promote God's kingdom, celebrities promote Satan's kingdom. Although God's stars are disciples who are exalted because of their humility, Satan's celebrities are initiates and only get exalted after they have been humiliated. Fraternities, sororities, Masonic organizations, and other secret societies are full of people who have humiliated themselves for the sake of obtaining influence. Some are naïve, but some know this influence comes from Satan, and they are willing to do anything to obtain it, especially movie and music celebrities. Aside from secret societies, many of them seek influence from shamans and witches that have favor with dark powers to release influence. Glory-seeking celebrities will do anything for epidemic popularity and fame.

It amazes me how they can thank Jesus at award shows for their songs about sex, drugs, and murder when God did not promote them; Satan did. They merely took God's gifts and used them to build Satan's kingdom.

Witchcraft Influence and Music

Deuteronomy 18:10 says, "There shall not be found among you any one that maketh his son or his daughter to pass through the fire, or that useth divination, or an observer of times, or an enchanter, or a witch" (KJV).

How does this work? Remember the group Three 6 Mafia? When they pose for pictures they are usually throwing up the devil's sign, made popular by heavy metal. Isn't it strange the favor these guys have? For years, their songs have glorified death, violence, lewd sex, even Satanism. They straight up promote destruction. But why did Viacom give them an MTV reality show, "Adventures in Hollyhood"? Why would the Academy Awards give its most coveted award for Best Film Score to Three 6 Mafia? Usually, a composer like Henry Mancini, Philip Glass, or Quincy Jones wins. These hip-hop thugs actually won an Oscar for their rap called "It's Hard Out Here for a Pimp"! Internet message boards have talked about Three 6 Mafia's song "Stay Fly," in which you can hear a young lady singing in the background that Lucifer is her god and her king. Just before Juicy J raps, he says, "Lucifer" faintly, then, "Lucifer" loudly. They actually invoke the devil's presence into this song! I know they thank Jesus in their award shows and say they only rapped about the devil to draw attention to their group, but that does not undo the damage they have done. As a matter of fact, many of their parents are actually preachers. Three 6 Mafia's talent may come from God, but their influence comes from Satan. Spiritually, isn't it obvious why they got such a platform for influence? It is because they have favor with the fallen star, once named Lucifer, and their influence, like the flu, is making our youth sick. Remember, influenza and influence are related words. Worse than the bird flu or swine flu, spiritual epidemics spread through music can destroy a generation.

Many hip-hop artists use witchcraft, voodoo, and spiritualism to gain epidemic popularity. Do you know that witches have actually been hired to "pray" over recording artists and their recording sessions in order to captivate people? Remember, that is part of the testimony from Kevin, former member of Color Me Badd. Witches summoned demons to be with the song "I Wanna Sex You Up" in order to captivate young people when they heard the song. Also, it's been revealed that Jennifer Lopez at one time was paying $75,000 a month to a spiritual witch doctor in Santeria for influence in this generation.

Parents, ever wonder why you cannot tear the poster down? Surprised you cannot take the artist out of your child's life? Isn't it strange, when you tell him, "No, you can't listen to that," your child does not stop? Could it be that the reason he goes right behind your back and plays sinful secular music is because there are spirits drawing him into it? Perhaps, depending on the artist, if the music has demonic influence. Satan is still in the music business.

Earth, Wind, and "Fires"

The most popular R&B music band ever is Earth, Wind & Fire. The group, known for its positive messages and great rhythm and horn section, has its songs played every five minutes on some radio station in America! This was one of my favorite groups, but when I began this ministry, the Lord revealed the "Reasons" for their epidemic fame. (Sorry, I know my "Reasons" play on words hurt somebody's feelings who played it at his or her wedding. But even one of Earth, Wind & Fire's leaders, Philip Bailey, said, "I can't believe Christians got married and danced at their wedding to our song 'Reasons.'" He said, "Don't they know, they just cursed their wedding? Because the song is saying after all is said and done, there are no reasons after all." And there you are in the shower, and even at church, squealing out "Reasons"! Anyway, I digress).

There is a video called "The Behind-the-Scenes Look at Earth, Wind & Fire," which details the inspiration behind their music. From this and other research I have seen, there is no way our church choirs and Christian musicians should play this stuff in church. Unfortunately, Kirk Franklin appears on the *Interpretations* album for Earth, Wind & Fire with secular hip-hop/"Neo Soul" artists and did a remake of the song "September."

Some might say, "What's wrong wit dat?" I'll tell you what's wrong with it.

Maurice White, during Earth, Wind & Fire's beginnings, was into yoga, meditation, and studying the world's religions. White took a pilgrimage to Egypt and studied Egyptian mythology and received inspiration for the name of his group, Earth, Wind & Fire, from the calendar of Osiris. Osiris is the god the Egyptians believed to be the god of all gods. Osiris had a calendar that his followers believed could manipulate time. Maurice White was into astrology, and his zodiac sign is Sagittarius, which he found had a primary elemental quality of fire, but also had seasonal qualities, which are earth and air. This explains why they left out water.

I mentioned earlier that Maurice White and other members of the band practiced yoga, which is Sanskrit and means "to yoke, or unite." In biblical meditation (Psalm 1, for example), you meditate upon the Word of God and ponder God and His majesty and fill your mind. In yoga meditation, you empty your mind in order to unite, or yoke, yourself spiritually to false gods, which supposedly promise peace and oneness with the universe, and make you a channel for their power. Of course, these are just demons masquerading around as angels of light (see 2 Corinthians 11:14). Why is this important? Maurice White said that the way he got his songs was through meditation and channeling Egyptian spirits!

You see this influence in Earth, Wind & Fire album covers. For example, in their album cover for "The Promise," you see the calendar for Osiris, with many Egyptian religious symbols. You also see the Black man with his hands raised, worshiping the sun god Ra. What you will see on his back, is many times mistaken to be a cross, but it is not; it is an ankh, and it's connected to Egyptian false god worship. That is not the "Black man's cross," as some have said. It is a demonic Egyptian symbol that predates Christianity.

On their album cover for "All in All," when you look to the left you will notice the third eye and the pyramids. You also see the shining star at the top, and you see Osiris and Isis coming together, of course, to create the supreme Egyptian god. These two and many other of their album covers contain astrological and zodiac symbols. Most people thought, *Awe, they're just going back to the Blackness,* and didn't understand what they were doing. To get the lyrics to their songs and the funky melodies that you love so much, they were channeling Egyptian spirits. Some might say, "Well, this was just all about Egypt and Black consciousness; what's the problem?" These are the very same Egyptian false gods that Israel was delivered from! As a matter of fact, modern-day Satanism as we know it was influenced by these same spirits. Aleister Crowley (1875-1947), who formed many of the philosophies for Satanism, was perhaps the most demonic man that has ever lived, and still influences Satanism today. Crowley said he had a spiritual encounter when he went to Egypt, in which he and his wife channeled Horus and Osiris. These evil spirits wrote through him a book called *The Book of the Law,* which makes up most of Anton LaVey's *Satanic Bible.* Why is this important? Listen: These are the same demonic spirits that were the spiritual inspiration for Earth, Wind & Fire's album covers and music. You might say, "But their songs were so positive and uplifting. What's wrong with dat?" This is not about positive or negative, but it is about source.

We forget there were two trees in the Garden of Eden. One tree was the Tree of Life; the other was called The Tree of the Knowledge of Good and Evil, which represents independence from God, rebellion, self-reliance, self-worship, and, ultimately, worship of Satan. If you read too fast, you missed a very important point. You see, the knowledge of evil and good are on that same demonic tree! You see, the same spirits, from the same demonic tree, influenced Aleister

Crowley and Maurice White. But the same holds true with today's hip-hop artists. Recently, I was informed of a very well-known, positive-sounding neo soul artist, who literally shut her concert down, she said, because she had offended Osiris! Satan wants you to rebel against God's life and seek life, good or bad, positive or negative, from his kingdom. New Age self-empowerment and other false religions are just the so-called "beautiful" side of evil.

I just picked an Earth, Wind & Fire song at random, sitting in my office one day, and thought I'd look at the lyrics, and boy, was I surprised. In the song, Shining Star, the reference to future roads is a reference to horoscopes. So the shining star is . . . astrology. He's talking about astrology. He's talking about looking to the stars for guidance. The adventure of the sun in this song is referring to the sun god Ra, who, in the song they say we should listen to its words of heat Ra. Understanding this helps you see the influence of their song "Serpentine Fire." "Serpentine" means serpent-like. The serpent that is like fire is the fallen dragon, Satan, in Revelation 12.

Observer of Times

Now, some of you say that's just a song, but you must understand that death and life are in the power of the tongue. When you sing these songs, you're actually prophesying this stuff. Once again, the devil knows you are not going to ask the sun god, "What am I supposed to do tomorrow?" but he knows that if he puts it in a song, he can influence you by manipulating your consciousness. This song was all about looking to the stars for guidance. But you know I've got to go to the Scriptures on this one. Deuteronomy 18:9-10 says, "When thou art come into the land which the Lord thy God giveth thee, thou shalt not learn to do after the abominations of those nations. There shall not be found among you any one that maketh his son or his daughter to pass through the fire, or that useth divination, or an observer of times . . ." (KJV).

What's an "observer of times"? An "observer of times" is that person who reads his horoscope and follows astrology. That's the person who uses the stars to manipulate his destiny or his purpose. That's the person who opens up the magazines, buys the scrolls at the counter at the grocery store, and uses that foolishness to get his lottery numbers, and other things, as a ridiculous form of guidance. Do you know that Christians do this stuff? They read their horoscopes and open up fortune cookies and say, "Oh, my fortune cookie said something good today." Deuteronomy 18:11-12 (KJV) says, "Or a charmer, or a consulter with familiar spirits, or a wizard, or a necromancer. For all that do these things are an abomination unto the Lord: and because of these abominations . . ." (Do you know what that means? That means, Don't do it!) Remember, Deuteronomy 4:19 says, "And beware not to lift up your eyes to heaven and see the sun and the moon and the stars, all the host of heaven, and be drawn away and worship them and serve them" (NASB).

Though Satan lost authority, he still has powers, and his music ability did not change. The Scriptures would have informed us if he was transformed during his fall, but he was not. He was an instrument in heaven, and guess what? Satan is still an instrument. He is still making music, and he is greatly using music to gain control of the minds of people. Remember, Satan influenced one-third of the angels to turn against the very presence of almighty God. How is that for influence! How did he do that? What gave him the power to persuade perfect angels standing in the perfect presence of God to rebel against God and be defiled by Lucifer? I believe that it was his music ability. Most of us do not understand how powerful music is. Music is the most powerful channel for influence.

The Power of Music

God began to reveal to me exactly how powerful music is. I knew the devil was evil, but I never pegged him as a musician. Nevertheless, when I started thinking about it, I began to see a pattern of destruction in people that are very talented in music and excel to be legends in the music industry. From Jimi Hendrix and Janis Joplin to Notorious B.I.G. and Pimp C (who died from getting high on drinking cough syrup and codeine, a mixture he rapped about called sizzerp), death, drugs, sex, and sinfulness all plague musical artists.

Music is not confined to the boundaries of our interpretation. Music is truly the universal language. Ever notice how people do not have to understand the lyrics of a song for their mood to be affected by music? Music can convey the lyrics without understanding the language because of the powerful way music is laced with mood-altering ability. God also told me that "Music can go into the mind of man and disturb his very conscience without his consent." Powerful!

I began to realize that without any effort, people can be taught with music. They can actually learn things that may be difficult to retain without music. For example, the jingle by Folgers coffee, "The best part of waking up, is Folgers in your cup," is known by nearly everyone, and yet people do not even remember the day they learned it. It's as if it just got into their being without their putting forth any effort to learn it. Now, when they think of waking up for morning coffee, they hear the jingle and reach for the Folgers cup! How about this one? Complete the last phase of this song: "Plop, plop, fizz, fizz, . . ." If you are over thirty, you probably said, "Oh, what a relief it is." Alka-Seltzer does not run this commercial any longer, but you probably finished the last phrase anyway! It is because music goes in, and it does not come out. This is effective advertising at its best, but there is a spiritual element to this that most advertisers will neglect to tell you.

You see, when a jingle is played into your subconscious, it is accepted by the frontal lobe of your brain. Once it is there, it unites with your perception, and whatever images are recorded from that point on will be associated with the music. The music basically plays the images and lyrics into your brain, so they all associate with one another. From that point on, when you hear that song, you will remember the images, and the images will remind you of the good or service that was attached to the jingle.

Dr. Roy H. Williams has a book called *Thought Particles*, and in this book, he talks about the function of the two hemispheres of the brain—the right and the left. He suggests that the left hemisphere of the brain is your conscious thought, logical analysis, and outer awareness, and it uses methods and rules that have been learned and accepted by you. He suggests that the right hemisphere is your subconscious thought, emotional reactions, and inner awareness, and is influenced by things such as creativity and music. The most powerful part of his research was his finding in effective advertising.

He found that when something is advertised visually, the right brain may accept it, but the left brain acts as a guardian and accepts or rejects it based on the rules and methods that exist in it. Yet, when something is put to music, it has the ability to go into the right brain, bypass the guardian or rules of the left brain, and influence both hemispheres of the brain. This proves not only what God spoke to me, but also how powerful the enemy can really be with music. The very place that the devil is most effective is with the God-given ability that he possesses, and that's music!

The Bible also speaks of Lucifer having a timbrel in his body. A timbrel is a percussive instrument, like the tambourine, that produces rhythms. Now, what makes music more powerful is a repetitive, strong, rhythmic beat. We can learn things much faster when they are put to a rhyming pattern and attached to a beat. Look at how you learned your letters of the alphabet. The letters were put to a rhythmic, rhyming pattern and easily taught to you. You not only remember your ABCs, but you retain the melody and rhythm of it, too.

When used like this, music can be one of the most effective tools for remembering important things and is often used in our school systems to teach fundamental things that must be retained for years to come. Most things put to this pattern will never be forgotten, and that shows us that music is very powerful. Music can unite people to a shared experience in history better and faster than any other influence. This is why Adolf Hitler, one of the most demonic men who ever lived, said, "Give me the music of the youth of a nation, and I can take that nation." Music can set the mood for an entire generation, creating the spiritual climate that will eventually change society.

The catch comes when there is a hidden agenda in the things that we are retaining through music. This is how the devil is able to deceive so many of us, because we feel that music can be listened to and the lyrics can be separated from the music. But because of the research that we have done, we have come to find that even though you do not want to retain the lyrical content, it comes with the music, and you cannot separate the two. Again, music goes in, and it does not come out. In addition, because your frontal brain takes mental pictures and creates images based on what is received through music, you cannot stop visualizing what you are listening to.

This is why there are far more radio stations in the world than television stations. Radio can do what television cannot. People watch TV, and the images are already created for them, so it does not cause them to visualize much on their own. If the images are created, then you only have to watch and enjoy them. However, with radio, the images are not created, and you can visualize with your imagination. This creates a more personal attachment to what you are hearing because you are able to substitute what you are hearing with what you are imagining. And since you can draw from your own repertoire of images (people you know, people you admire, things that are dear to you, and so on), radio keeps you involved and massages your creativity while giving you a more lasting impression. That being understood, just imagine what effects negative music has on the listener and the negative things that the music will pull out of these subconscious thought processes.

It's almost as if music reinforces many things that a person would really like to forget and covers up things that should be retained and remembered. Music actually can act as a catalyst for negative reinforcements as well as positive ones. Think of it this way: There is not a greater force in the earth, other than the power of God. Yet, even God requests your permission to influence you; He stands at the door and knocks (Revelation 3:20), while a musician does not. God needs your agreement to work through you and change you, but a musician doesn't! Music can totally bypass your psyche and teach you, influence you, and change you without your even being aware of it. Your mood can be altered, your decisions can be swayed, and your whole life's journey can be shifted by the content of the music you listen to. This is why cultures and subcultures always develop when there is a strong musical influence present. As you can see, people are led into subcultures because of the powerful influence of certain types of music.

Depending on the content of the music, the subculture will emerge as a life practice of the music's content. People will begin acting out what the music is relaying to them, and they will act as living manifestations of the music they enjoy. What really happens is that the music becomes a channel for a belief system and is used to transition a way of thinking, into a way of life. You see, the belief system is always here first, and the music just becomes the advertisement or the marketing strategy of the belief system.

For example, when the devil wanted the free love, free sex hippie subculture of the sixties, he raised up The Rolling Stones, The Beatles, and The Doors. When he wanted marijuana, cocaine, and heroin to go to another level, he raised up Curtis Mayfield, Rick James, and George Clinton of Parliament Funkadelic to fuel the drug subculture in the seventies. And when we wanted to incite rebellion and Black empowerment, he raised up Bob Marley the Rastafarian; Earth, Wind & Fire; and eventually, Afrika Bambaataa, to create a Black Consciousness Movement in the eighties, knowing it would eventually give birth to hip-hop as a subculture. From sex and drugs to Black empowerment, music became the vehicle for transmitting the ideas and influence of these movements.

A nuclear physicist can say, "No more nukes!" and nobody will say anything. But a high school dropout rock celebrity can say, "No more nukes!" and thousands of people will frantically shout it with him. As you can see, music can influence far more people and does not need their permission!

Fans, Followers and Worship

So the devil knows, if he wants to indoctrinate a people with corruption, all he has to do is raise up a music celebrity "superstar" in a subculture, because a fan is a true follower. (When God spoke this to me, it just blew me away.)

A fan is follower, and a follower is a worshiper. Biblically, a worshiper is not someone who just sings a song to God, but someone who gives his body and being over to God. Romans 12:1 says: "Therefore I urge you, brethren, by the mercies of God, to present your bodies a living and holy sacrifice, acceptable to God, which is your spiritual service of worship" (NASB).

Biblically, we are being changed into God's image and likeness spiritually as we behold Him. The beauty is, what you behold is what you become, which is the highest expression of worship. You behold God in your Bible quiet time as you meditate on His goodness. You also behold God in prayer. When you do this, you take on God's characteristics and you worship Him not just in a song on Sunday or Wednesday night, but you live a lifestyle of worship. You "look" like Him because you begin to act like Him in situations. His power and love manifest through you, and because you love Him, you are a living sacrifice willing to sacrifice or lay your life down for Him. Unfortunately, the same can be said of the followers in Satan's subcultures.

You can always tell true followers in a subculture, because weeks after the concert is gone, they are still emulating the leader. In other words, it might be three weeks since the concert, but they are still wearing the spiked gloves and the tour jackets, or they have new tattoos similar to their favorite artist! They become what they are beholding, which is the highest expression of worship. For those who understand this, their logic is, *"Why speak a message, which can be challenged by the guardian, or left brain, when you can put the message to music and have both hemispheres of the brain influenced by it?"*

Music subcultures are used by Satan to change the spiritual climate of nations. The hippie subculture, with Luciferian groups like The Doors and The Rolling Stones, ushered in the free love, free sex psychedelic subculture that brought in LSD, heroin, and other drugs. Later, just as Satanism targeted the rock music of the 1980s and used it to preach their message, we now have a religious subculture of hip-hop that has targeted music as a way to preach a non-biblical, self-worshiping doctrine that is pushing the youth and young adults of our day further and further away from Jesus Christ.

Once I was preaching in Los Angeles, and the concert ticket sales for one particular well-known secular hip-hop artist were slumping. The record company thought it might have to do with what I was preaching, against hip-hop, so they sent one of their publicists to hear me. God, however, had another agenda in mind. The publicist sat through the entire message and came up at the altar call at the end. She repented, and got saved and filled with the Holy Spirit! She asked if she could address the audience at the end of the service, and she began to tell who she was, why she was there, and how God set her free that night. She told everyone, "What he is preaching is true. I've been in rooms where recording artists are signing their deals, and witches and shamans are praying over them. I have seen witches in recording studios, calling down lust demons so the artists can have influence in their songs. Please pray for these artists, like the one I represent. Though he says he is a Christian, he has done this very thing and used witches to cast spells while he was recording in the studio. But now he has a problem. He has a sex addiction that is out of control, and he is seeing a psychotherapist because he cannot stop having sex with the men and women in his group." How sad. But then again, of course, he is struggling with homosexuality and other identity issues because the devil does not play fair. You cannot defeat what you have embraced.

I also have received phone calls from executives in the music business, looking for a way out of the business. One actually told me that whenever there is a new album released, a party is thrown, and witches come in and invoke principalities, and ask their demons to go wherever the songs on the album are heard. Another told me that finished master recordings of these albums are placed in pentagrams, Satan's star. Yes, even the masters for the Christian gospel artists that are signed to major record deals, he said, were placed in pentagrams in the mastering facility and offered to Satan. This same executive said that at one meeting he was in, the Christian gospel artists who were signed to their label played their finished albums for them, seeking their approval before they released the project. When the gospel artists left, the music company executives laughed and said, "It's a sad day when God has to use the devil to get His music out." This information came from people who were promoted to some of the highest levels in the music industry. Once they found out about this realm, they were frightened, but because they loved their six-figure salary so much, most looked the other way and would not quit. Which would you rather be, the world's celebrity on your way to hell, or God's star on your way to heaven?

Chapter 9

Look Familiar?

Heavy metal music had a large following and still does, but I do believe that it was only an introduction to what the enemy really was planning for our generation. He wanted greater numbers, and heavy metal just could not draw the large followings because of its loud, chaotic sound. People who were musically inclined or who just appreciated good music were not drawn to heavy metal music. In addition, people who had basic decent morals were turned off by heavy metal because of its satanic undertones and graphic, explicit content. I remember God speaking to me and telling me that there was a subculture, or belief system, that was about to be promoted through a form of music that was on the uprise. Satanism was attacking our youths through many of their star hip-hop recording artists, and it was happening so subtly that no one was really seeing it. Hip-hop artists like Snoop Dogg and Bone Thugs had all kinds of satanic elements in their music. There was a religious connotation to them, and they didn't mind promoting their dark sides in their lyrics.

After that, I started paying close attention to the artists who were being introduced during this era, and I began to see the plan of the devil in action. DMX, whose name has been said to mean Dark Man X, surfaced around this time, and his music was like a mixture of hard-core hip-hop music laced with heavy metal antics. He was loud, rude, explicit, and demonic, and did not care what anyone said or thought about him. I read that he supposedly made the same deal with Satan as Snoop. I do not remember exactly where I read that, but when you look at his lyrics and consider that he did a song with Marilyn Manson, it's not hard to consider that a possibility. But DMX is hard-core and blew up in the industry overnight. He is raunchy, nasty, and very violent in his lyrics, and has a criminal record in real life. I guess with him, as with many new gangsta rappers, life resembles art in almost every way. One of his CDs is titled *Flesh of My Flesh, Blood of My Blood*, which basically mocks the blood of Jesus Christ and his holy Communion. On the cover of this CD, DMX is covered in blood from head to toe!

If you were to see the album cover, you would clearly see his name is strategically placed above his head in large letters so that the "M" in his name rests upon his head. The empty spaces in the letter make it look like he has horns upon his head like the devil. This was definitely not an accident, but intentional because the content of this CD is very explicit. There is a song on the CD that was popular, and made the phrase "Ya'll going to make me lose my mind, up in here," even more famous. I have even heard preachers in church repeating this phrase, acting as advertisers for this explicit recording artist. However, the saddest part of that is, the song is very graphic in depicting homosexual acts between men in prison! I warn pastors and preachers all the time of the dangers of trying to use familiar sayings and clichés like these to be relevant. They do not understand that they are promoting the very thing that is destroying the mind-set of their youth.

In addition, don't think these guys that make this music are not applauding the church's promotion of their music. But DMX even considers himself a preacher and plans to start a church one day. However, his music should be played in the church of Satan because of how sexually explicit and violently vulgar it is. As I mentioned before, he even has a song with Marilyn Manson on one of his CDs. For those who do not know about Marilyn Manson, he is so perverted that he is said to have removed a portion of his ribs so that he could perform oral sex on himself! At the end of all of His CDs, DMX always does a song where it sounds like he is praying and talking about God. Do you know that some Christian parents buy the CD because DMX talks about God at the end of his CD?

Listen to what DMX says in a *Vibe* magazine interview:

"Tonight has been an exorcism, you understand, as DMX is plagued by demons. People believe you can only catch the Holy Ghost in church," he explained weeks earlier. "No, I get it on stage. I'm like a superhero," he says. "You know? Like a preacher of rap. I'm a savior. I'm the voice of those that have no voice. I see who they are, who we are. I'm their voice. . . ."

We must realize that this is all antichrist. Anything that is against Christ or the opposite of His teachings is antichrist. The Bible tells us that the spirit of the antichrist is already here. In addition, just as it used heavy metal music to promote the goth subculture, it is now using rap music to promote the hip-hop subculture! And there are so many artists out there now that are straight up anti-Christian in their lyrics, appearance, and beliefs, and they are promoted, endorsed, and marketed by the recording industry with no restrictions. What God revealed to me is happening now on a large scale, and it seems that the world is silent about it.

Ja Rule is another hip-hop recording artist who uses his music to preach false spiritual doctrines, and his music even changes the words of the Bible and perverts the very truth that we know today from the Word of God. Ja Rule has a CD titled *Rule 3:36*, which is a mock of the biblical passages found in John 3:36. But he actually took Scripture from the Bible and flipped it around to mean something totally different from what God was speaking through the Word. We know that the antichrist spirit is already here, and it comes to twist the truth of God into a lie. It comes to disturb the very foundation of truth and cause the people of God to become confused and deceived by making the truth and the lie so similar, that unless God reveals truth to you, you will believe a lie! The Word of God says it like this:

And for this cause God shall send them strong delusion, that they should believe a lie: That they all might be damned who believed not the truth, but had pleasure in unrighteousness.
2 Thessalonians 2:11 KJV

Ja Rule has a CD cover where he is breaking two biblical commandments at one time. He is posing in front of a church, exposing his tattoos on his back, which are angel wings around two crucifixes. His name started out to mean the initials of his name with the word "rule" to mean in charge of, but now he is playing with the Word "Ja," saying that it stands for "Jah," "God" in Rastafarianism, which is idolatry and false god doctrine. So on this CD cover, his name is stating that he is a god, and he even has two crosses in his name. The first biblical commandment of God's ten commandments that He gave to Moses is: "Thou shalt have no other gods before me" (Exodus 20:3 KJV).

On this same CD cover, he has two golden "god pieces" hanging from his neck. These represent gods and what God is supposed to look like. They are golden idols that many rappers wear, but Ja Rule wears two of them, along with two crosses. Ja Rule says one cross represents God as God, and the other cross represents him as god. This also goes against commandment number two, which states that:

Thou shalt not make unto thee any graven image, or any likeness of any thing that is in heaven above, or that is in the earth beneath, or that is in the water under the earth: Thou shalt not bow down thyself to them, nor serve them.
Exodus 20:4 KJV

Ja Rule has lyrics that contradict the Bible intentionally. I'm not talking about the fact that it promotes sin, but I'm talking about specific, intentional rewording of the Bible and changing it to mean what it was not intended to mean. This is heresy and false god worship to anyone who listens to and enjoys his music. His music is against God, yet many who listen to and enjoy his music claim to be down with Christ and the Bible. This is ridiculous because if you believe the Bible is the Word of God, then why would you, or how could you, enjoy a man who takes Scripture out of the Bible and changes it like a heretic for his own beliefs' sake? Are you mad? How can you justify even absorbing antichrist lyrics through your enjoyment of his music? That is insane, and if you think you can serve God and listen to and enjoy the musical teachings of false god worshipers at the same time, then you must have never read this Scripture:

> No man can serve two masters: for either he will hate the one, and love the other; or else he will hold to the one, and despise the other. Ye cannot serve God and mammon.
>
> Matthew 6:24 KJV

In the words to the song, "Only Begotten Son" by Ja Rule, he takes John 3:16, and changes it to put himself in it as a god! He is speaking it as though he is the way to God and he is the Christ! But in the second stanza of this song, he states that God "so feared the world!" Now, this is crazy because he directly went against the Bible and stated something that is opposite of what the real Scripture states. The Bible says:

> For God so loved the world, that he gave his only begotten Son, that whosoever believeth in him should not perish, but have everlasting life.
>
> John 3:16 KJV

Now, you can see that he changed the word "loved" to the word "fear," but why? Well, if you know the Bible—and I believe the devil knows the Word because he quoted the Scriptures on many occasions in Bible history—you would realize that the Bible says:

> There is no fear in love; but perfect love casteth out fear: because fear hath torment. He that feareth is not made perfect in love.
>
> 1 John 4:18 KJV

So, according to the Bible, fear is the opposite of love! But Ja Rule stated the opposite here because he is opposite of, or "opposing," God. His lyrics and even his name are antichrist, and one of the deceptions of the antichrist is totally changing the Word of God to speak something that it did not intend. Opposite of God is anti-God, which is antichrist. Furthermore, the Bible says in St. John 1 that God, Christ, and the Word are one in the same. Therefore, when a person attempts to change the words of the Bible, they are opposing Christ and can be considered antichrist. It is this anti-Christian system that the devil is using to steal all evidence of truth from our youths. They hear false Scriptures and doctrines preached through their music, and it confuses them. God is not the author of confusion, but the devil is the master of it. Therefore, while they are receiving these mixed religious messages, they are accepting and worshiping these artists as gods in their lives, and it makes it impossible for them to truly serve the true and living God. The devil knew that he could do these things through music and create a godless generation without any resistance because music is so powerful. Through the power of music, our youths are suffering while being influenced to turn their backs on the truth of God and accept the false gods of hip-hop in rap music. Artists like Lil Wayne, Lil Jon, Ice Cube, 50 Cent, and many others promote false god doctrines in their music, but it seems the hip-hop subculture is subtler and is the least resisted, even by born-again believers! I guess the religious undertones or the mentioning of God in the music causes many believers to be blinded and subscribe to the doctrines of false god worship in this music without even knowing it.

What most people do not realize is that hip-hop music is not just promoting the doctrine of hip-hop, but it is also promoting the doctrine of self. The knowledge of self, or the doctrine of self-deity, is an age-old mentality that puts a man in God's place. Realistically, anyone who is not born of God or into the kingdom of God is a self-worshiper because he is choosing his own flesh over the sacrificed flesh of Jesus. The Bible tells us:

I beseech you therefore, brethren, by the mercies of God, that ye present your bodies a living sacrifice, holy, acceptable unto God, which is your reasonable service.

Romans 12:1 KJV

This is telling us that in order to really come to God, you must first deny your flesh, or your own way, and choose Christ's way. Through the blood of Jesus, we can come to God, and through His sacrifice on Calvary's cross, we can have eternal life through Him. He died for our sins, and if we accept this, we can have life eternal. But the only way to God is through Jesus Christ, and by no other name can men be saved but through the name of Jesus, according to the Bible. This is why the doctrine of self-righteousness or self-worship is so dangerous, because it totally deletes the true way to God and makes us, and not the God of gods, our own master. If we are our own master, then we cannot serve the true and living God because no one can serve two masters. Well, the attitude of hip-hop is the same as the attitude of heavy metal was. It's self-promotion, self-glorification, and self-worship. It's the attitude that our inward expressions should be manifested outwardly and we should show ourselves, promote ourselves, and worship or please ourselves because we are in charge of our own paths. This is why rebellion is key, because you defy God's plan and follow your own way. It's just like witchcraft because in hip-hop, you do what you want, live like you want, and look like you want, regardless of whether it's appropriate, readily received, or accepted by leadership.

Hip-hop has the attitude that every man is responsible for his own way, and whatever god he chooses is acceptable. If you pay close attention to it, you will find that hip-hop music is not about the music, but it's about the way of life that these guys subscribe to. That is why you can't just enjoy hip-hop music without subscribing to the lifestyle of it. If you embrace the music, you are embracing the artists and their beliefs. After all, how can you separate the artists from their beliefs if they are preaching these beliefs in their music? Hip-hop, the subculture, was founded on the principle of self-rulership and self-expression, so the music can only follow suit. The music is the preacher, or messenger, for the religious beliefs. Therefore, since the hip-hop subculture was not founded on Christian values, but self-consciousness, it can never glorify God. Because it is a self-glorifying, self-expressive movement, we know that it is not a promoter of the truth of God, but actually a nemesis to the Bible and the righteousness of Christ. Why? Because if self is the focus and self-expression is the objective, then Christ cannot be the end result because the Bible says:

> Then said Jesus unto his disciples, If any man will come after me, let him deny himself, and take up his cross, and follow me.
>
> Matthew 16:24 KJV

I am not saying that a person should not have an outward expression of his gifts or talents, but I am saying that a person cannot choose his own way, but God has to be the only way.

People who accept the subculture of hip-hop as their governing factor will not be led to God, but will be led to self-worship and self-rulership. You cannot deny yourself if you are promoting yourself. You cannot deny yourself if you are governing yourself. You cannot deny yourself if you are promoting the sins of the flesh because sexual sins of the flesh are forms of self-worship. Choosing to pleasure yourself sexually, outside the boundaries of marriage, is self-worship. This is why hip-hop promotes sexual sin, the love of money, and the doctrine of self as god because these are all self-serving devices that are the opposite of Christ and His way. Hip-hop is an antichrist in this regard because it opposes the truth of the Bible and makes the way of man another acceptable way to God. Let's look at some of the self-serving doctrines that hip-hop promotes more in-depth so we can understand the plan of the devil to deceive our nation's youth even more.

Chapter 10

Sexual Sins

Throughout history, sexual sins have always been destructive to a person, nation, or culture. In fact, unlike lying or stealing, sexual sin is against the very "body" of a culture. In other words, it affects the body of a person as well as the corporate body of a culture. When a culture, or people group, subscribes to sexual sin as a norm, you can always expect a detrimental end to that group of people shortly thereafter, due to the negative impact of sexual sin to a body of people. And every subculture that has ever used music to promote itself almost always promotes or exploits sexual perversions as a marketing strategy. You see, appealing to one's carnality is the easiest way for Satan to infiltrate a person's course of life.

First Samuel 15:23 says, "For rebellion is as the sin of witchcraft, and stubbornness is as iniquity and idolatry. Because thou hast rejected the word of the LORD, he hath also rejected thee from being king."

This is what witchcraft does and why rebellion "is as the sin of witchcraft," according to the Bible. The devil wants to get a person to be stubborn and refuse wise counsel. He wants to set a person up to fail, and usually he does this with a natural act that God has deemed good, yet he twists it into something that can destroy the path of a person. Such is the case with sex. The devil wants to take the good act of sex and pervert it so that it costs people their very lives. This undermines and destroys a culture of people.

Dr. Meg Meeker, in her book *Your Kids at Risk: How Teen Sex Threatens Our Sons and Daughters,* outlines the following alarming statistics:

- This year, 8 million to 10 million teens will contract a sexually transmitted disease.
- Nearly one out of four sexually active teens is living with a sexually transmitted disease at this moment.
- Nearly 50 percent of African-American teenagers have genital herpes.
- Although teenagers make up just 10 percent of the population, they acquire between 20 percent and 25 percent of all sexually transmitted diseases.
- Herpes (specifically, herpes simplex type 2) has skyrocketed 500 percent in the past twenty years among white American teenagers.
- One in five children over age twelve tests positive for herpes type 2.
- Nearly one out of ten girls has chlamydia, and half of all new chlamydia cases are diagnosed in girls fifteen to nineteen years old.
- Sexually transmitted diseases accounted for 87 percent of all cases reported of the ten most frequently reported diseases in the United States in 1995.

The alarming reality, according to Meeker and others who track these numbers, is the figures by now are actually many times higher. Now, doesn't this make you want to turn off BET and MTV, and clear your radio settings from any hip-hop stations? If not, it should! What starts the cycle to these alarming stats? For starters, let me share my story.

Since Satan feared my future, he used a few adult women in my church to molest me and do lewd sexual things to me when I was a young boy. I believe this to be the reason most of my generation is sexually dysfunctional, because their sexuality was "awakened" at a young age by being exposed to sex or molested as a child. Molestation, rape, incest, and other sexual sins are being perpetrated upon our generation so frequently that it's hard to trust our kids with other people for any period of time. Parents, beware! Be careful of the places and people that you allow to watch over your children. Spending the night at friends' and some family members' houses could be an opportunity for the enemy to make his move on them. You see, he is targeting their youthfulness because he wants to disrupt their innocence and cause them to harbor secrets at a young age. When a youth hides things, it's like an initiation to a lifestyle of hypocrisy! Once the youth masters the art of hiding things, he or she will eventually graduate to lying severely. The person will learn to live a double life, and the enemy will use this to distort this person's perception of life and walk with Christ later in life. This person will always hide things and never fulfill God's commandment to "confess your faults one to another, and pray one for another, that ye may be healed" (James 5:16 KJV).

True healing happens when we are able to confess our faults, or issues, to someone. As long as we hide it, we will never be delivered from it. So we do not want our youth to ever have to harbor sins that were perpetrated upon them because this gives way to a life of hiding and untruths. That's why it's good for us as parents to keep an open line of communication with our children so that they will not be afraid to talk to us about things that they feel are private or secret. We also need to make sure that we as parents aren't hiding things from our past because this will only cause us to become closed about ourselves, and thus close the door on our children's opportunity to share with us. We have to guard our youths and protect them, for the enemy's plan is to expose them to sex at an early age and awaken their sexuality before they are old enough to manage their feelings and emotions.

Molestation or rape introduces young children to their sexuality at an early age and causes them to begin making adult decisions with a child's mind. This also explains the rise in homosexuality and lesbianism. Almost every homosexual I have ever ministered to was molested at a young age by a male figure. I believe young people become confused about their sexuality after being molested by a person of the same sex. The experience causes them to question their sexual preference. For instance, if a girl is molested by a woman, then she begins to question why the woman was attracted to her. Then she begins to believe that she is a lesbian because she thinks she attracted a female or believes something about her caused a woman to want her. The Word of God says, "as he thinks in his heart, so is he" (Proverbs 23:7).

Because Satan used women to molest me, I began to think that I was a playboy, and a player, since I had grown-up women wanting me, and I was only around ten years old. At first, I felt like something was terribly wrong. I could feel my adolescent eyes being opened and my sexuality being awakened. God later showed me that our bodies mature only as quickly as our minds allow. That is why so many of our young people these days are maturing so fast physically. Teenaged girls have adult women's bodies, and teen boys are getting facial hair and a man's physique at a younger age. Their bodies are maturing fast, and they are developing at a rapid rate. Many experts say that the growth hormones and preservatives in our modern-day diet can explain this phenomenon. I believe that these are only partially responsible.

Most of the accelerated maturity is due to our young people being exposed to things that their minds should not be entertaining. Movies, videos, books, and, of course, music are exposing our youths to adult situations and themes at a young age. In addition, as they are exposed, their minds are causing them to think adult thoughts and causing their bodies to mature accordingly. Your body will mature as fast as your mind does. When a person's body does not develop properly, this person usually has a brain disorder. He is retarded, and he functions as a child because his mind does not mature. Well, when a person is overexposed to adult situations, sex, and images, his body develops too quickly and it causes him to have an adult mentality in his teen years. He begins to act out adult behaviors, while retaining his teenaged understanding. This is one reason we are having so many behavioral problems with our millennium teens.

Many of them are trying to have adult relationships and are making life-shattering mistakes because they do not have the right mind-set to be seriously involved with another teen. This is why I discourage boyfriend/girlfriend types of relationships between teens and adolescents. Any type of relationship they get into will, almost always, move too fast because they are pressured by our society to behave like adults. How can we expect our teens to be responsible enough to behave properly in a "love" relationship with their peers when everything around them is pushing them to become physical and go all the way? I strongly believe that parents and youth leaders should beware and never endorse any kind of boyfriend/girlfriend type of relationship among teens in our time because there just are not enough positive reinforcements for them when they pursue these types of relationships.

Generational Cycles

When a young lady gets pregnant at an early age outside of marriage, it causes that child to be born into a deficit. That child will grow up and usually commit the same sin because he is deficient in the same areas as his parents, inheriting his parents' poor mind-set regarding promiscuity. This generational cycle repeats itself, creating a culture of deficient people who use other things to make them feel sufficient because of their natural void. For example, if a child is born into a home without a father, that child will substitute the father in his home with another leader. And almost every time, the leader he chooses is HIMSELF! He replaces the governing power of the man in the home with his own rules, ways, and desires.

We must understand that this is how the subculture of hip-hop was born. Because of the lack of men in the home and the accepted norm of sexual behavior outside of marriage, children were born in great numbers without the presence of a father figure. As a matter of fact, nearly 80 percent of African-American children grow up in single-parent homes, many of which are fatherless. Naturally, this deficit produced children who idolized other images, adopting their idol's beliefs and values to govern them. As you can see, hip-hop was created by these people as a tool of self-expression that gave these youths the confidence they lacked because of their development without a governing, father-type leader. Hip-hop became the father substitute, mind-set, and governor for these youths. And because hip-hop has a self-serving mentality, self became their focus as well.

Remember, all subcultures that are birthed within another culture usually are birthed because of some sort of lack or deficit. Subcultures usually promote rebellion as the norm to negatively empower the low self-esteem of their insecure members who were born into lack. God is the supreme Father, and because He is able to recreate us, He can become our Father, or Governor of our lives, but we must accept Him and His ways. The dilemma is that once a person subscribes to a belief system birthed out of his lack, he must denounce the beliefs of the false father image in order to embrace and fully receive the benefits of God as his Father. Otherwise, he will be double-minded, unstable in his life, as he attempts to serve two masters. This, of course, explains the unstable lives of hip-hop artists who thank Jesus at the Grammys, but live immoral lives. It's no wonder that they privately struggle with drugs and suicidal thoughts, and are in and out of rehab and jail. As you can see, if hip-hop or the gothic subcultures are accepted as tools for self-governing, then when you become Christian and choose God, you must let go of all other governing principles and choose Father God's ways alone.

Another reason why the enemy promotes sexuality so much in hip-hop is because this gives birth to lack. Sure, the artists who are performing or promoting it have money, but most of them still have no fathers in their homes or have low self-worth outside of their talent and stardom. You take the money and fame away, and they do not even feel good about themselves. This is because they grew up with lack and never accepted God as a replacement for their fatherlessness. They, like their followers, turned to a subculture, or belief system, that acts as an artificial father-type leader—hip-hop. But the truth of the matter is hip-hop has failed as being the father they lack because they continue to struggle with acceptance and low self-worth. How is this recognized? We see this through hip-hop's promotion of material things, selfish behaviors, immorality, and money in the place of upstanding values and morals.

This is proof that their lack of a leader and father has taken its toll on them. All of this is because someone misused his God-given sexuality for self-glorification outside of the marital bed. God was not trying to stop his fun, but He is trying to stop these cycles from being born. The bottom line is that God wants people born into homes with a mother and a father! We are beginning to think that the mother's role is the only important role in a child's life because we see it so often. The truth, however, is that God divided the seed and egg to require both parents for childbirth. Listen, this indicates there is something in the man and the woman that the child needs and that is required to exist sufficiently. The father's role is just as important and necessary as the mother's. And when the father is not living in the home with the child, the child will suffer lack in many areas. As a result, he will search for replacements that may lead to a lifestyle of substitutions and inferiority.

Do you see why the enemy produces this cycle? You see, the sexual behavior that is promoted in hip-hop is present to birth more children who will grow up in lack, which, in turn, promotes the agenda of Satan to destroy the dominant culture by the reproduction of lack from its subculture. As a result, the more children who are born without fathers in the home, the greater the decline of values in society. The greater the decline of values and morals, the less likely the society will survive, because of murder, crime, sexual perversion, disease, and abortion, which are all birthed through sexual sin. You see, the devil plans these things from early childhood. His strategy is to cause a seed of sexuality to be planted in a child by molestation, rape, inappropriate touching or fondling, incest, or sexual abuse. Once this seed has been planted, then the devil will wait until the proper age of discovery in the life of the child or teenager to introduce that person to a life of sexual perversion.

Masturbation, homosexuality, promiscuity, and other perversions are then introduced through the seed that was planted earlier. Later comes the life of hidden acts of secret sexual sins. Next, when these people reach the age of self-governing, the enemy will always introduce them to a favorite musical artist, which ultimately will lead them into a subculture of people who practice the sins they practice. As you can guess, the artists they become attracted to are into the same sins they are hiding. It's like a pied piper: The people in the subculture are led astray by the music and the sin promoted in it, only taken into a deeper downward spiral of sin. Their mental anguish about their struggle is acknowledged in the music, without any solutions being offered. The music then leads the person into the subculture's belief system or doctrine, governed by people who all struggle with or are bound to the same types of sin, resulting in the sins becoming second nature and an accepted norm by the group. For example, jazz/bebop music was a catalyst for the beatniks. Heavy metal was a catalyst for the gothic subculture. And now rap music is a catalyst for hip-hop. The beatniks, the goths, and now the hip-hoppers all promote sexual promiscuity as normal behavior. Sexual sin is part of their subcultures because all of them subscribe to extreme self-expression. And the ultimate selfish act one can perform is self-pleasure through sexual perversion. When you commit sexual sin, you are pleasuring yourself and becoming a "god," or governor, of your own actions rather than being led by God. These subcultures all promote illicit sexual behavior as the norm and digress from biblically structured sex between a married man and woman. This is why you see almost all artists in our nation's music industry promoting some sort of sexual behavior outside the confines of marriage.

In hip-hop, women are exploited, sexuality is worshiped, and lewd sexual behavior is entertaining. This is why artists like Snoop Dogg, 50 Cent, and Nelly all have porn videos and websites that promote their pornographic materials. Sexually explicit behavior and hip-hop go hand in hand because it's all self-glorification and self-worship. In our history, every man who considered himself "god" would have no sexual act denied him. He could do whatever, with whomever, with nothing refused him. This is supreme self-worship and a "god" complex because it shows that you are in total control of another person when you can make that person submit to you sexually. And because hip-hop promotes the doctrine of self and the "self is god" mentality, sexually explicit behavior is the norm. When people subscribe to hip-hop, they will always struggle with illicit sexual behavior.

The father of lies through hip-hop will create generational curses that will go for three, four, even ten generations (see Exodus 20:5; Deuteronomy 23:2). You see, the curse of having children out of wedlock goes to ten generations because it is rooted in rejection, and perpetuates sexual sin, pain, and loneliness. But the culture of the kingdom of heaven, ruled by Father God, releases generational blessings that go to a thousand generations, which means, basically, forever. The truth is that just as you resemble your natural father, you will resemble your spiritual father's mannerisms and way of life. Think about it: If your father is Satan and hip-hop subculture, you will look like the father of lies. On the other hand, if your Father is God through Jesus Christ, your mannerisms and way of life will resemble the heavenly Father. Spiritually, you cannot obey two fathers. Who's your daddy?

Chapter 11

Momma's Boy

As a young teenager, before I ever had a reason, I was waking up early. Believe me, at first it wasn't my initiative. It was my father's idea. He started waking me up early because my father believed I needed my own money and needed to learn to work at a young age. When I turned thirteen years old, he made sure he woke me up before he went to work. I remember asking him one morning why I had to get up so early during the summertime, since I had no school. He responded, "No man needs to be asleep past 7 A.M. If I gotta get up, you gotta get up!" I remember being real dumb and saying, "But I don't have anything to do!" What was I thinking? He did a "Joe Jackson" on me and messed up some stuff outside, just so I could fix it! I never made that statement again. This was the end of boyhood and the beginning of manhood for me. He started looking for a job for me, and a year later, I was working at fourteen years old.

My father, along with being a pastor, worked for an apartment complex as a maintenance man. My father got me a job cutting grass and doing some landscaping in the complex where he worked. I remember that first day of work like it was yesterday. I was riding in a truck with an ex-convict named "Quick-draw" and another guy who smoked weed all the way to work. I was in the car scared to death, and I held my breath all the way! I couldn't wait until we got to the complex to start working, just so I could exhale! We laid train track crossties in the apartments that day, and it was about a hundred degrees outside! I was burning up and working like a Hebrew slave, but on the way home, I had a feeling of accomplishment, and it felt good. Even though part of me didn't want to go back, I felt like I had done something, though I was covered in soot and blackened by the sun. When I got home, however, my mother screamed when she saw me. I was a mess, and she yelled, "Come here, baby" and started hugging me and giving me her emotional nourishment. As soon as she did this, my whole attitude about accomplishing something went out of the window! I started buying into her care and quickly jumped on her side of things. She started saying how I was not going back and that was too much work for me. She told my father that I was quitting and I wasn't going back the next day. My father calmly walked over to us and separated us and said in a very calm, but authoritative voice, "He's going back tomorrow," and that was it. I was like, "But Daddy, heed the voice of the woman!" But he wouldn't budge, and he made me go back the next day. This was a pivotal moment in my rearing because had he not been there, I would have fallen in an emotional trap set by my mother. Of course, my mother wasn't doing anything that women are not wired to do. She was being a nourisher and emotional, like all women should be. But the balance of the man was important in establishing my ability to work and take care of my family one day. My father saved the day and wasn't even aware of it. He was just being a man for me to see, so that I would know how a real man handles responsibility. There are many cases when my mom's emotional nature was needed to soften my dad up so he would not be too harsh with my sisters or me, but this was one time when her emotional reaction needed to be countered. What if my father wasn't there? More importantly, what happens in the lives of young boys when fathers are absent and hip-hop replaces them? Could it be that forty years later, they're convicts called "Quick-draw" or smoking weed and going nowhere in life? In this important chapter, we'll discuss hip-hop's negative impact of fatherlessness on the Black community.

I believe one of the greatest casualties of the lack of Black fathers in the home is women confronted with the challenge of raising boys without the example of a man in the home. Women are able to nourish and nurture any child, but when it comes to making boys into men, there seems to be a problem in our Black households that consist of women only. From what I've observed, what tends to happen is the role of a mother is overemphasized, and when the man is nonexistent, the father's role is de-emphasized. This causes an imbalance, and the boys are left to fend for themselves when it comes to adopting male role models and leadership. As a result, gangs, the streets, and, more prevalently, hip-hop becomes the outsourced identity that is accepted and act as the father filler for our young boys who desire male leadership.

The Importance of the Father

The role of the man in the home cannot be overlooked and left to chance. This is a very important role, and it must be filled. It cannot and will not be nonexistent, and will get filled by whatever means. One way or another, young boys will find male leadership, but unfortunately, when left to a teenager's mentality, this role will usually be filled by pop culture's iconic leaders or the social networks of the communities that surround our young boys. This is where hip-hop finds its way into the hearts of many of our young men. If you look at the rise of hip-hop in our world, you will see something else that has risen with its numbers. As hip-hop rises, so do high school dropout rates, imprisonment, teen pregnancy, and the like. But these are all consequences of the fatherlessness in the homes of our young Black men. Kids seek to outsource the role of their fathers, and this poses our problems.

From what I've observed in many years as a teacher and a minister, and working with youth, when a boy is raised primarily by a woman, without a man in his life, that boy will lack male strength in many cases. In many cases, I've seen single mothers resort to emotional manipulation in an effort to impose their will upon their older sons to keep their attention and respect. She feels she has to control her son somehow; therefore, she resorts to emotionally manipulative means to dominate him. What she doesn't realize is that, inadvertently, she emasculates her son. Without having a father in the home, the young boy will sometimes struggle with identity and gender confusion (almost turning into a girl, in many cases), so that he will respect the mother as a mother- and father-type authoritative figure. This presents many problems for young men in our society. They get a false worldview and don't really understand the authority of a man. As a result, when men are placed over them (school teachers, employers, policemen, and so on), they tend to rebel and feel dwarfed by the authority of a man. They get so acclimated to the voice of women that they fear the voice and authority of men, in most cases. This causes them to abandon situations that require them to submit to male leadership. They quit jobs and school, and rebel against the law, in many cases, because they can't endure the authority of a man. This explains why many times, the young man that grows up with a father deficit prefers to submit to a woman's authority, because he experienced in his dysfunctional upbringing a distorted, one-sided view of leadership.

There are two distinct roles that should be implemented in every home: The mother, nurturing and feeling; and the father, disciplinarian and male validation. These two roles are very important and should never be overlooked or substituted. They are essential in the development of a child and will play a very important part in the life of a child, as he or she becomes an adult in our society. The mother is the nourisher. She takes care of the child during his or her younger years and emotionally connects with the needs of a child. She can feel the child's needs and, in many cases, protects the child's feelings and emotions because of her emotional nature. This is important because it gives the child a sense of care and concern for others. The way the mother handles this role will determine how the child responds to care and nurturing for the rest of his or her life. A child gets this from his or her early years in the care received from his or her mother.

The father, on the other hand, has a very important role as well. He is the disciplinarian, and his lower, deeper voice is a signature of authority and implants a certain fear and reverence in the life of a child. This sets the stage for the child's sense of authority and respect for leadership. This is the example of how we should fear God. The way a child fears the voice of his or her father is not a scary type of fear, but a reverence and respect kind of fear. This is very important because if this is missing during child rearing, then the child may grow up with a false perception of authority, and the fear is not reverent, but it is a scary fear that will be felt toward male leadership. When it's this type of fear, it usually causes rebellion, avoidance, and rejection of authority. What are the consequences of this?

Young boys are dropping out of school, not working, and not going to church because they do not want to experience the fear of male leadership they have, based on their own lack of experience with male leadership. In other words, they would rather avoid those situations altogether, in most cases, than endure a man's commands and demands. Such is the case for most young people who have never experienced true male leadership: Reverence is replaced by fear, and they avoid authority, rather than submit to it.

Another role that the father plays in the life of his child is male validation. Men give a child validation from a leadership standpoint. In other words, since God made man the head of woman, as Christ is the head of the church, the man is in a greater position to validate the child. This is not an insult to women at all, but it's a fact that is stated in the Word of God. And any true godly woman is honored to allow a man the role of leader. So the image and likeness of the man give validation and affirmation to the child. This is very important to young boys and how they perceive themselves. Their strength really comes from the example of the father. They learn how to be men, how to care for their families, and how to rule their homes well. They get their validation for life from the man that is placed in the home as an example. In the same manner, we get our validation for life from Jesus Christ, as He is placed in our churches as the head example for our living. When the man is not in the home or in the life of the young boy, he does not see an example of the way he should go, and this causes him to either abandon being a man altogether (homosexuality), or rebel and become an emasculated momma's boy that only responds to the voice and leadership of a woman. And this is where emotionally led men, thug images, and the prison homosexuals termed "jailhouse fags" come from.

He-motional Man

When a father is not present in the rearing of his son, the boy, in most cases, will miss a vital example. Now, don't get me wrong; I'm not saying that this is present in every man who is raising his son, but it definitely is supposed to be. What I'm referring to is the man's ability to deny his feelings and conduct himself as a man, free from making emotional decisions or acting based on feelings, rather than logic. The truth of the matter is that men should be able to control themselves and not react to emotional circumstances and feelings. When things go wrong, a real man can deny his feelings and act using logic and self-control. Even when angry, he can conduct himself in a manner in which he has no regrets later and can be proud of his ability to suppress his emotional reaction. This allows him to make good, sober decisions and fix problems. Men are inherently problem-solvers, and we should attempt to solve the problems and deal with our personal feelings later. Women are emotional creatures, and they act on emotion. This is why the Bible calls the woman the "weaker vessel" (see 1 Peter 3:7). This is not about physical strength only, but it's referring to her emotional nature and how she is inclined to make many of her decisions based on her emotions. This is a very good thing when it comes to raising children, loving and caring for her spouse and family, as well as countering the man's logic and problem-solving initiative. This balances out the man and gives him "help" when it comes to softening up or setting his logic aside when needed. Men need women to do this. But a woman needs a man to balance out her emotional nature as well. Without a man in the home, a woman will raise a boy and exhibit emotional imbalances before him. This can hurt him as he is reared because he will have no concept of logic, problem-solving, and reasoning without emotional interference. He will see and experience a one-sided view of problem-solving. If he only sees the emotional reactions of a woman as a model for decision-making, consequently, he is more likely to become a man led more by his emotions. This becomes very dangerous to him because if not balanced, this can lead to a life of having male authority and dominance without self-control and discipline. In no way am I stating that women are without self-control or discipline, but what I'm saying is that a young man needs the stability of a man's reasoning and logic, coupled with the emotional nature of a woman, to have balance in his future. If there is no man present in his life, then the young boy will become too emotional, and this doesn't work well with his male-dominant nature. This, in most cases, turns to anger and uncontrolled exhibitions of frustration and wrath. In a lot of cases, I've seen this lead to a life of crime, violence, imprisonment, and moral failure.

Our dropout rate among African-American teenage boys is 75 percent and rising. Why? Because when you have an emotional young man who is angry at life or wrathful because of his absentee father figure, many times you will have a young man who is a ticking time bomb. Once he is pushed past his boiling point, he will react emotionally and not rationally. He will walk away from challenges and abandon situations that he feels he cannot control. Instead of "manning up" to trials and sticking it out, he will quit. He will run to his mother in shame and submission. And rather than having a man telling him to "be a man," he will, in most cases, hear, "That's okay, baby; it's going to be all right." There is a balance that is needed today in the lives of our young boys and girls, but with a 50 percent divorce rate and nearly 80 percent of all Black youths being raised by a female only, this abnormality is fast becoming the norm in our communities. This is a problem, people, and now it has fast become THE problem that will end our African-American society as a whole if we don't change things.

Our Black young men are quitting jobs, school, and the like these days because they have no motivation at all to stick it out. They have no male telling and showing them that they are to be a man. A woman cannot teach this. A woman can raise a boy, but cannot raise a man! There must be a positive male figure in the lives of our boys who can show them how to do life. They need to see a man sticking it out and being a man when it gets tough. They need to see a man obey the law and uphold truth at all costs. They need to see a man without compromise living by conviction, who knows that wrong is never right and right is never wrong. They need a man to show them how to take care of their families and not run from responsibility. They must have a man in their lives that they can see treating women with respect and honor, and not depending on them for their needs, but being a man and taking care of the woman's needs for security, provision, and protection. How will they know if they don't have the examples to show them? Is hip-hop teaching this?

Sins of the Fathers

When a strong man is not present in the rearing of a young boy, and this young boy is governed by emotions and anger toward his father, this, in turn, produces wrath. The Bible tells fathers to provoke not their children to wrath (see Colossians 3:21), yet this is being done constantly by fathers abandoning their families or not being responsible when it comes to their children. This causes young men to lash out in rage and anger. They join gangs, commit crimes, and become menaces to society because they have problems dealing with the wrath that is in their hearts. The saddest part is that wrath, in most cases, causes them to do exactly what was done to them! For instance, they walk around upset at their fathers for not being there to raise them, or not being in their lives to take care of their mothers. Eventually, out of wrath, these same young boys sleep around carelessly, making babies they don't father, with women they don't take care of. Wrath only reproduces itself and if not dealt with properly will lead to a life that will, in most cases, land them in jail. That's right, jail is fast becoming the Black man's vacation. As mentioned before, in 1980, 143,000 Black men were imprisoned in America. As of this writing, in 2008, there were more than a million, and that number is rising. Black men, who make up only 6 percent of the population in America, account for 50 percent of our prison population! And this has caused some crazy things to happen to our young Black males that are not in prison.

The Bible teaches us a lesson in Genesis about how the son is made in the image and likeness of his father. The Bible tells us that God created us in His image and His likeness. In other words, He gives us identity and an image to emulate. We get that from God Himself as His sons. Well, the Bible also talks about Adam giving birth to Seth and his being created in Adam's image and likeness. This is what happens to our children and why they look and act like us. They take on our image and likeness because they are born of us and come from us. This is natural and spiritual as well. The

Bible teaches us that the sins of the fathers will revisit the children (Deuteronomy 5:9), and that what the Father does, we do also when it comes to the works Jesus performed. You see, fathering has spiritual consequences. What the Bible illustrates is the fact that we take on not only the physical character of our fathers, but the spiritual things as well. The Bible even goes on to say that the promise of redemption is for our children and our children's children. And the bastard curse, when a father is absent, can go on for ten generations spiritually, if not addressed and dealt with (see Deuteronomy 23:2). I know I'm throwing a lot at you, but you must grasp this to understand the next point I'm about to make.

If you throw a million men in prison, what happens to their sons? If we take on the character of our fathers, and their character is that of wrath, vengeance, and violence, then what of their sons? It is a known fact that most Black men in prison who want to escape sodomy must pledge their allegiance to Allah and confess him as their god. Well, we know that Allah is not the God of the Holy Bible, but he is fast becoming the god of imprisoned Black men. What does this do to their sons? Well, most gangs preach and teach Allah as god to their gang members. The sons are learning what the fathers are pledging and not even making the connection, yet in the spirit, the connection is strong. While all these men are turning to the false god Allah in prison, their sons are turning to him in gangs and other organizations, as they join for leadership and camaraderie. What is this doing to our young boys? It's causing them to lose their desire to learn about Christ and the Bible, and turn their affections to Allah. This is why Blacks in America are the fastest-growing Islamic conversion community. Blacks are converting from their traditional views and accepting the lie of Allah and Islam at an alarming rate. And because of this, the violence of Islam and Muslims has begun to plague our communities even more.

Now, the teachings of killing, murder, and suicide are fast becoming the themes of our rappers and entertainers. Don't forget that the founding fathers of hip-hop say that hip-hop rests upon the teaching that Allah is god. So it doesn't take a rocket scientist to come to the conclusion that this is all a great setup by our enemy, Satan, to create a lawless group of young warriors for Allah who will deny that Christ is Lord of all and resort to violence and self-infliction to prove it. Wake up, people! This is the real deal.

Jail and prison are celebrated in hip-hop, and a rapper can gain street credibility by getting arrested and doing time. This is the driving force behind the hip-hop industry. Being a gangster or criminal is celebrated, and jail is where criminals go, right? So it's no wonder that the influence of those behind bars is growing in our communities. You see, the young boys you see every day are looking like their imprisoned fathers more and more. The sins of the fathers are again revisiting the children, and their imprisoned fathers are altering even the appearance of our young men. The look that has become the style among young Black men is now becoming the norm. It's not abnormal to see a young Black man with both ears pierced or wearing a doo-rag out in public while sagging his pants and showing his underwear. It's very common to see a shirtless young man walk the streets, showing his underwear and tattoos. It's the style now for a young man to wear cornrows and fancy braids, even with beads and barrettes on the ends. What about the men who wear ponytails and bangs? Males wearing earrings and getting their ears pierced is so common these days that even infant boys are getting them done. But this did not start all of a sudden or overnight.

In the Bible days, earrings were used as symbols of slavery. Slaves were tagged on their ears for identification and ownership. Later, in the Egyptian culture, the mark of two earrings or multiple piercing on a male represented bisexuality and whorish behavior. And all the great kings and leaders of godless civilizations who were lascivious wore them to symbolize sexually immoral behavior.

In the early seventies, pimps started wearing one earring in the Black community as a symbol of slavery to sex. It meant that you were a player and enjoyed multiple sex partners. It was called "macho" from the term "machismo," which means "excessive male or extreme male." Also, one earring meant you were homosexual, depending on which side you wore the earring, mostly determined by which region of the country you were in. This is what the single earring meant and still means: a whorish man or a homosexual man. Two earrings on a man was, and, in most cases, still is, a symbol of bisexuality. And now, since our young Black boys are emasculated and becoming very effeminate because of the lack of fathers in the homes, the two earrings are taking their age-old meaning once again.

It's not uncommon to mistake a young boy for a young girl these days, and vice versa. This is becoming commonplace in our communities, and the lines between males and females are being blurred. Haven't you noticed how even younger kids have started to look like she-he hybrids because of the braids, beads, and earrings? Why is all of this becoming so popular all of a sudden? Well, this is nothing new, but because of the jail influence on our young Black males, the sins of the fathers are again revisiting the children.

Prison Subculture

If you remember prison movies in the seventies, you will remember the term used back then and still today to describe the flamboyant homosexual man, the "jailhouse fag." This is the man that the prisoners would experience woman-like relationships and sex with. Because there are no women in the male prison for prisoners to fall in love with and have relations with, they had to emasculate a man and turn him into a woman so they could have a woman-like man to have sex with. Men in prison usually force themselves upon the younger, weaker men, but when the sex is welcomed, and they have a man in prison who desires their sex, it makes them feel more normal than with rape and gives them the illusion of being with a woman. Somehow, this gives them some sick, morbid feeling of sexual freedom, and is used to answer their fantasy of sex with a woman. As you can see, "jailhouse fags" were made to resemble the former girlfriends of the other inmates, to somehow make them think they were not homosexuals. Consequently, this caused many homosexual men to be adorned as women in jail to fulfill the fantasy of being with a woman that many of the inmates had in the outside world. So they took homosexual men and deconstructed their image further, changing them into feminine creatures by first braiding their hair in cornrows. You see, braids in Africa are for women, and they began wearing them in America in the jails. The cornrows (a Nigerian hairstyle that showed the coming of age of young girls) entered the Black male community through prison. Stronger men emasculated other men when they sat under them to have their hair braided. They sat between their legs and allowed these men to braid their hair as a symbol of being a slave to, or being sexually dominated by, the men they were sitting under. You see, braids were a step to turn a male into a female in prison. When the man didn't have an adequate length of hair, they improvised. They would force him to wear a doo-rag that would hang like a woman's hair or tie a bandana around his head like a woman's head wrap. Also, he would be forced to sag his pants to show his underwear as a teaser for sexual enticement. The sagging was a sexy look for the so-called "jailhouse fag" to turn the inmates on sexually because it was like wearing lingerie. They would make him either tie his shirt under in the front (like Tupac did and other effeminate rappers do now), or wear no shirt at all to show off his physique and tattoos. Something else that was considered sexy for inmates was for "jailhouse fags" to wear a "wife-beater" (a sleeveless tank top undershirt), making it look like a bra or underwear of a woman.

Does this sound familiar? Just a few years ago, this was the look of a prisoner who had his masculinity taken from him and who turned into a socially impotent male in prison, and now, if you visit your local school, mall, or anywhere young boys go, you will see the same look. The "jailhouse fag" is the look that many of our boys are modeling. Most of them, not understanding what braids, sagging, and other symbols mean in prison, though not physically imprisoned, are preparing for prison by emulating the look of their imprisoned and socially impotent fathers. Once again, the sins of the fathers are visiting the children, and hip-hop is the catalyst for it all. In the next chapter, we will look at hip-hop's false doctrine of greed.

Chapter 12

The Love of Money

In hip-hop, the love of money is promoted. We know that the Bible says this:

> For the love of money is the root of all evil: which while some coveted after, they have erred from the faith, and pierced themselves through with many sorrows.
>
> 1 Timothy 6:10 KJV

What makes this Scripture really applicable to our society? It is the fact that whenever a person is lifted up and placed in a position to really govern or affect the lifestyles of people, and a lot of money is involved, evil will always be prevalent. You see, the devil targets people who will do anything for money to govern people who do not have money. If a person has no integrity and will sell sex or sin for money, then that person will be lifted up in this country because that means, as we learned in the previous chapter, that that person is self-serving. A self-serving person who will do anything to be famous or rich has an internal issue of low self-worth. In other words, this person will not allow God to give him security in his purpose through Him, but rather, he will make his own way and seek riches to give him security in this life, rather than the gain of godliness. When the Bible says you cannot serve God and mammon, or money, it is really saying that you cannot seek God and money. You cannot go after both. Sure, we all want to be successful and work hard for money. But the problem comes when people lose their integrity and sell their own conscience for money. When they commit sin to get money and have no integrity with their riches, then they are serving money, rather than God. Most people in our entertainment industry sought after fame and riches to get where they are. This is why their lives are plagued with sin. Even in Christianity, men have sought after wealth and riches and compromised their integrity to get it. Gospel recording artists have signed contracts that made them take Jesus and God out of their songs, record with sinful secular artists, and even sleep with men and women to get promoted to stardom status. There is a difference between worldly success and godly significance. It's the same all across the board: If you will do anything to get it, you are mastered by it!

In the Bible, there was a man who was caught up in his money and power, yet he wanted to get to heaven. He came to Jesus and asked Him how he could have eternal life. This man had everything in this life, and people knew of him as a great man. He was arrogant and high-minded and was only asking Jesus this question so that he could have "everything" that life and death had to offer. Let's look into this story and pull out his true motives. Look at what he first said to Jesus:

> And, behold, one came and said unto him, Good Master, what good thing shall I do, that I may have eternal life?
> Matthew 19:16 KJV

Now, we can see in this Scripture that his motives were not right. First, he said to Jesus, "Good Master," and this offended Jesus because he was speaking to Jesus as if Jesus was a god, and not *the* God. This is common for people who have exalted themselves above others. They want to believe that they are in good with God, and because of what people think of them, God must feel the same way about them. It is like bringing God down to their level because they are so lifted up in this life. Money will do this to a person. Because people feel that they are great, and they are lifted up as gods themselves by people's perception of them, they will try to find a way to bring God to their level. He called Jesus "Good Master" to mean that he could have direct and swift access to God because of his position. Then he said, "What good thing shall I do for eternal life?" He was not asking Jesus for eternal life, but he was trying to prove that he already had it! He was really saying, "I have done everything right, so, tell me that I already have it so these people around us can hear it." How prideful! He was not asking for it because he said, "What good thing . . .?" and that shows us that he was not speaking from the standpoint that it was something Jesus could give him. This is arrogance, but it's very common because when people are lifted up in this life, in the flesh, they begin to believe their own hype, press, and what people are saying about them. And when they have a lot of money, it makes it even harder for them to stay humble and reverence God without reverencing themselves.

Matthew 19:20 says, "The young man saith unto him, All these things have I kept from my youth up: what lack I yet?"

Here the young man gets really arrogant and brags about keeping all the commandments all of his life. Now, this was a straight-up lie; it is impossible for any human to accomplish this. Yet, because of his money and position, he had ultimately persuaded himself that he was worthy of eternal life. But check out what happens next. Matthew 19:21 (KJV) says:

Jesus said unto him, If thou wilt be perfect, go and sell that thou hast, and give to the poor, and thou shalt have treasure in heaven: and come and follow me. But when the young man heard that saying, he went away sorrowful: for he had great possessions.

Here, Jesus speaks right to the problem. Jesus knew that it was the money that was making this guy act this way, and therefore, He told him to give it to the poor. He was really telling him that he needed to exchange his earthly wealth for treasure in heaven. In other words, He was saying, "Do not chase money or allow money to master you, but let money chase you, and you master it!" If the love of money is the root of all evil, then the only way this man could get to see God was to deal with the "root" of his problem, his money. Now, do not get me wrong; I am not saying that we should not have money, but I am saying, if your money was earned through compromise, sinful acts, sin promotion, or any other corrupt means, then you should give it away and allow God to, as His Word says, give you the power to get wealth! Deuteronomy 8:18 says:

> But thou shalt remember the LORD thy God: for it is he that giveth thee power to get wealth, that he may establish his covenant which he sware unto thy fathers, as it is this day.

Had this man obeyed Jesus, he would have prospered in Jesus and not only had spiritual prosperity, but he would have prospered naturally, without the arrogance of self-gain and self-promotion. Notice what Jesus said after all this:

> Then said Jesus unto his disciples, Verily I say unto you, That
> a rich man shall hardly enter into the kingdom of heaven.
> Matthew 19:23

This is why we see such a mixture of religion, gods, and spirituality in hip-hop and other music forms. People are trying to justify the desire to be famous or rich, and they want to cover up their feelings of betrayal and compromise by praying in their songs, talking about spiritual things, and referring to themselves as "Christians," while all along promoting sex, sin, and lust. That does not make sense, yet this is one of the oldest of hypocrisies. You see, people create a Jesus in their own minds and hearts who accepts their lewd behavior and sinful lifestyles. They think their way of life is justified because they are some kind of superstar in the flesh. As a result, they live by a different set of standards than the Bible. They think that if their good works outweigh their bad works, then they're okay with "the big man in the sky." Our Christians are even buying into this, and megastar Christian recording artists and superstar preachers are now living all kinds of sinful lifestyles, believing that Jesus understands and that because of their fame and money, they can "fame" their way into heaven. But fame and good works will not hide their dark secret sins from God. What they need to hear is what the red-letter writing of the Bible says.

Jesus said that a "rich man," referring to men who have made themselves or consider themselves "rich," can hardly enter into heaven. When you go your own way and use sin to get money and fame, then you are rich from blood money. Your money is not from God, and you are not blessed! You are operating in a cursed state because you chose money over God, and the Bible tells us that you hate God if you love money because you cannot serve them both, and the mere fact that you want to serve them both says that you hate one of them. If you love the money, guess which one it is that you hate? This is why hip-hop artists and some Christian artists flaunt their money, fame, and lifestyles before men in magazines and television interviews. They have sold out their God and become as Judas was in the Bible. They sold out the truth of Jesus for money! They have gone their own way, living by their own rules, lording over their own selves for fame and money. What Jesus wants them to know is that His intention for the young man in the Bible is the same intention He has for them. You see, had he given up the sinful ways and the wealth he had from following his own way, he would have received God's wealth one hundred times more than what he had. Peter heard this and replied, "Okay, we gave up everything to follow You, Jesus; what do we get in this life?"

> Then answered Peter and said unto him, Behold, we have forsaken all, and followed thee; what shall we have therefore?
>
> Matthew 19:27 KJV

What Jesus says after this is what has driven my whole life. I have been blessed by God financially ever since I really understood this Scripture. Check out what my beloved Savior had to say to Peter and YOU about giving up stuff for Him:

And Jesus said unto them, Verily I say unto you, That ye which have followed me, in the regeneration when the Son of man shall sit in the throne of his glory, ye also shall sit upon twelve thrones, judging the twelve tribes of Israel. And every one that hath forsaken houses, or brethren, or sisters, or father, or mother, or wife, or children, or lands, for my name's sake, shall receive an hundredfold, and shall inherit everlasting life.

Matthew 19:28-29 KJV

What Jesus is saying is that if you give up sin for Him, you will receive your reward in heaven, and if you give up compromised prosperity, you will receive up to one hundred times what you gave up in this life! Isn't that amazing? What does this mean? Well, it means that you do not have to compromise for gain, but rather, those who do not or refuse to compromise for gain will get blessed with what they refused anyway! Not only that, but they will receive it from God and not man. And if it's from God, man cannot take it away!

People get on star search programs, such as "American Idol," and even have these competitions in their churches and other places seeking celebrity stardom and fame. They want to excel and become rich and famous. However, when they get it, it always causes them to sell God out because God does not see them as famous, as they see themselves. To acquire more wealth and fame, a person has to compromise his integrity (if he ever had any before; the jury is still out on that one), and he has to sell sin, sex, and lust because the Bible tells us these are all that are in the world. Therefore, to sell as an entertainer to the world, you must give the world what it wants! This is bleeding over into our churches, our Christian entertainment, and even our church leaders. They are seeking fame, money, and glory, but the end result is watered-down messages of prosperity, success, and "purpose-driven" lives instead of Jesus-driven lives! Unfortunately, many people want to be driven by prosperity, or self-gain, rather than by the truth of the Word and righteousness. Hip-hop is the greatest influence on our youth in our time, and because of this, the artists of hip-hop are promoting swift gain, no integrity, no boundaries, just making the money and getting the fame, no matter what it costs you. And now, our churches are mimicking it, and our youths are suffering.

The love of money also is promoted heavily in hip-hop because money is celebrated and hailed as the "way out" of poverty and lack. But the problem is that money may be an answer to financial poverty, but the lack of a father, the lack of leadership, and the lack of integrity, money is not an answer for. Yet, the hip-hoppers seek riches and flaunt their money in their videos and all over their bodies. Some even flaunt their gold in their mouths by covering their very teeth with gold. This is self-promotion at its core. Now we see young men wearing giant diamonds on their ears (mostly fake) and all kinds of jewelry to promote their own worship of themselves and their love of money. In the rap videos, cars are flaunted, houses are shown off, and money is hailed as the "have all to end all." But do not forget the words of the Bible: "The love of money is the root of all evil!" Even in Christian music, singers and artists flaunt their houses and cars on MTV and BET shows like "Cribs" and the fabulous life of so-and-so. Since when did it become necessary for Christians to show off money and riches? Many preachers on television preach the love of money while scrambling godly prosperity with financial gain, rather than the biblical principle of soul prosperity first and then financial prosperity.

> Beloved, I wish above all things that thou mayest prosper and be in health, even as thy soul prospereth.
>
> 3 John 1:2 KJV

God is concerned with us prospering in Him first before we get money. But the hip-hop subculture promotes quick and fast riches without morality and godly values. And the sad part is that while these artists prosper off their talents and musical skills, they are only a pawn in the devil's game to promote sin. So they may appear to prosper in the natural, but in the spirit realm, they are puppets with a greater purpose, and that is to deceive! How? They cause our nation's youths to mimic them in their daily lifestyles, but the appearances, the language, the behaviors, and so on, that these artists promote will only serve as blocks for the followers.

Chapter 13

God Complexes

It's interesting, you will notice that hip-hop artists are not mocking or quoting the book of Buddha. They are not trying to join forces with Hindu singers. They are making music with Gospel artists. Remember that I said the doctrine of hip-hop denies that Jesus is the Christ. So how do you persuade a Christian artist, who serves and worships Christ, to unite with a person who denies Christ? Maybe we should ask the self-proclaimed "pastor" of hip-hop, Hezekiah Walker, who is a Christian artist, yet his choir is singing background on a CD that contains lyrics that say that reading the Bible is irrelevant, and encourages people to open up their third eye vision, which is witchcraft!

Say what? How could a Gospel choir back a CD saying this? Now, recently, KRS ONE released a so-called "Gospel" CD, and it was in perhaps every Christian music store in America. He makes a point on the CD to speak much of God, but very little of Jesus.

How can an artist who does not worship Jesus become a Gospel artist? He openly states that he is a god. Isn't this unbelievable? In the 1990s, hip-hop really began to push its true agenda on our youth. In this chapter, we will discuss other spiritual origins within hip-hop.

As hip-hop groups began coming out, many were straight up preaching the doctrine of self-worship, or the whole "self is god" concept. Various groups began to surface that spoke of the Black man being god, and they carried themselves as if they were gods. Remember Big Daddy Kane? Well, the very name "Kane" was an acronym that stood for "King Asianic, No One's Equal." This phrase is used by Five Percenters to describe the true gods of this planet, "the original asianic Black man!" See how they hid that? Yet, many people followed the music of Big Daddy Kane, not even aware that he was claiming to be a god! Rakim even had faces of Black gods on his CD covers. On one of his CD covers, he had the four founding fathers (gods) of hip-hop giving birth to him!

This is how they really began to push their hidden doctrine of self as god through the music while all along deceiving their listeners into receiving and embracing them as just musical artists. Groups like Poor Righteous Teachers, Leaders of the New School, Erykah Badu, Outkast, Digable Planets, Black Sheep, Busta Rhymes, A Tribe Called Quest, and more began to take over the music industry while all along promoting this doctrine of self-worship and Black supremacy. White and Black America had no clue, but they were buying into a false god doctrine and worship system that was promoting antichrists from within the industry and causing serious spiritual damage to our youth and the followers of hip-hop. While dancing, partying, and just listening to this music, they were being changed. People lost reverence for God, the church, and the way of the cross, and they became self-serving, self-promoting, and self-righteous because their music was influencing them to accept themselves as god equals and govern themselves accordingly.

If music can influence a person without his permission, then music that preaches against Christ or the Bible will cause a person to resist Christ or lose his desire for reading the Bible. You see, these artists were a part of a doctrinal belief system that says that the Black man is god and Jesus Christ is the "white man's God." The Five Percent doctrine is a religion that was founded by a man named Clarence 13X, who was a former Nation of Islam leader turned self-god teacher. They believe that Jesus Christ is the white man's deception and way of influencing the Black men of the world into worshiping a "white" god. This sick doctrine sounds crazy to a true believer of the Bible, but do not be fooled. This is one of the hottest religions on college campuses, and music and movie stars follow Five Percent teachings.

Wu-Tang Clan

Now, the Wu-Tang Clan was one of the hottest groups in the country in the early 90's, but few people knew most of the members are Five Percenters. They used to have a video on their Web site, where the blade from their logo, the Wu-Tang, goes into a church and cuts the head off of white Jesus on the cross, then takes His Spirit and uses it to create the members of the Wu-Tang Clan! This is shocking! So why did they want to kill Jesus? Because they believe Jesus is the white man's God. If you are shocked, you should be, but they are not the only ones. This is what many of our Black entertainers believe, and their fame and money, to them, is proof that they are like gods or should be revered as gods.

Rastafarians and Dreadlocks

Bob Marley was a strong follower of Rastafarianism, and much of his songs about Jah and Zion and the Lion of Judah was Rastafarian doctrine. How did this religion get started? The Bible says there once was a very wise man named Solomon. Though Solomon was the wisest man and the richest man, Solomon did have one problem: jungle fever. Evidently, he loved the Black women from Egypt. God told Solomon not to go after the women of other nations because they worship and go after strange gods. He should have obeyed God and left them alone, but Solomon was like, "Yeah, but man, they are so fine!" God said, "Leave them alone," but it appears Solomon couldn't help himself. As a result of his disobedience, Solomon and the Queen of Sheba birthed a son. We know the Bible says that Jesus Christ was going to come out of the lineage of Solomon, from the house of David. In other words, the seed of David was going to produce Jesus Christ. This seed, or lineage, of David was in Solomon because Solomon was David's son, right? Well, Solomon took the seed and mixed it with a woman from Egypt and produced a false Christ lineage.

Later in history, a man came up in Ethiopia, who became the king of Ethiopia and was believed to be an offspring from Solomon and Sheba from Egypt. His name was Rasta Fari, and he later changed his name to Haile Selassie. Haile Selassie was the emperor of Ethiopia. A group of people emerged that worshiped him; they called themselves Rastafarians. The Rastafarians believe that Haile Selassie is Jesus Christ, the Black one! They believed this so much that they began to worship him and call him the lion of the tribe of Judah. As part of their religious practice, they believed in order to worship this false Christ, they must wear their hair as a lion's mane. So they started wearing their hair in a style known today as dread-locks. They wore dreadlocks to look like lions, in worship of this false Christ, who they believe is the true descendant of Solomon. That's what the whole dreadlock thing was connected to: false god worship. The Rastafarians are an anti-establishment, "down with the white man" subculture of rebels. They brought such anarchy and lawlessness wherever they went, people with "the dreaded locks," or dreadlocks, were not allowed to depart from boats and enter some Caribbean countries. You know, we cannot do everything the world does and call it a cool style without checking to see if there is a spiritual meaning.

Tattoos

Sacrificial markings are another way to worship, when writing somebody's name on your body. Isn't it weird how soon after a person gets caught up in sin, the person wants to get a tattoo? The person tattoos himself or herself in order to show allegiance to someone or something, but where does that come from?

Now, there are many hip-hop artists who have pledged their allegiance to something or someone, and want to display it. Many hip-hop artists have numerous tattoo markings and antichrist symbols. The Bible says in Leviticus 19:28, "Ye shall not make any cuttings in your flesh for the dead, nor print any marks upon you: I am the Lord" (KJV). Now, did I read it wrong? Let me read it again because churchgoers are still getting tattoos and calling themselves holy hip-hoppers. Let me say it again, "Ye shall not make any cuttings in your flesh for the dead, nor print any marks." Nevertheless, our kids sit at home and watch Bow Wow, Exhibit, and Faith, along with many other athletes with tattoos, not understanding the spiritual consequences.

The word "tattoo" is a Tahitian word, which means to mark something. The belief behind tattoos was that the wearer of the image summons the spirit of the person named or the image placed upon him. This is what happened in Egyptian culture. When God told them, "Do not mark yourself," the Egyptians actually marked themselves in order to call forth the spirit of whatever they wrote on their bodies. And they began to behave and act out those demonic spirits from whatever tattoos they placed on their bodies. For instance, if they tattooed a lion on themselves, they began to act or behave with a lion's spirit or a lion's demeanor. If they had the name of a dead person, that person stayed attached to them spiritually. Are you listening to me? Even today, when people mark themselves, the same spiritual principle applies because tattoos create spiritual soul ties to people and demons. Many tattoo artists consider what they do more than art. They even consider themselves priests, and the rooms where they tattoo, their sanctuaries. It's definitely spiritual for them.

Also, God does not want you to tattoo your body because when you mark yourself, it's just like a bookmark. It holds you at a place. It holds you right there so that every time you feel like you have made some progress, you will see that mark, and it takes you back. It makes it hard for you to live down what you did because there's a constant reminder, or mark. That's why Paul said, "I press toward the mark of the prize of the high calling, forgetting those things that are behind." You can't drive forward while staring in a rearview mirror.

Many times, when I pray for people with tattoos, demons manifest, and there is a fight for freedom. This is something that definitely must be renounced. Confess this sin before God, anoint your body where the tattoo resides with oil, and renounce the soul tie and spiritual connection you have with it. Though the tattoo may still be there, you can break the spiritual power and bondage to it. If you can pay to get it removed, it is worth your consideration. But look, I am believing for the all-powerful God to start dissolving this stuff off folks' bodies—off the bodies of folks who really, really want to get saved and want to live this stuff down and say, "I'm not the person that I used to be. If any man be in Christ, he is a new creature!" I'm just waiting for somebody to say, "My tattoo disappeared! It started fading off my body, and now it's gone!"

This is why trusting a music industry that is out to make money is so dangerous. It doesn't matter what a person sings about, believes, or teaches, the music industry is going to try to profit off it and promote it. It's all about money for the music industry.

Now, these teachers and religions have a platform that is better than any church, pulpit, or radio/television broadcast! They can put their beliefs in their music and cause the world to accept those beliefs subliminally, without being aware of it. However, the sad part is that listening to false doctrines and beliefs through music has the same effect as reading them or being taught verbally. It will change you. If you are listening to music with hidden passages of Scripture from the holy Koran like Jill Scott's song "A Long Walk" or KRS ONE teaching his self-god doctrine in his song by saying, "Reading of the Bible is irrelevant, you gotta look within yourself not a scripture," then what are you really doing to yourself? I'll tell you. You are accepting a false belief system in your life and, therefore, living under a curse. The Bible says:

> As we said before, so say I now again, if any man preach any other gospel unto you than that ye have received, let him be accursed.
>
> Galatians 1:9 KJV

If you sing, listen, or dance to music that contains a false belief system or false god doctrine, then you are accepting a cursed thing, and your life becomes cursed in the sense that you are confessing or receiving a curse through a false teacher! What does this produce? Well, if you are enjoying the false doctrine, you will not be able to embrace the true doctrine of the Bible. This is why some people can't read the Bible or understand it after they have read it. I know people who read whole passages of Scripture, sometimes entire chapters, and cannot remember what they read immediately after they read it! They have to reread it to even remember what they read. This is because the music has taught them a false god doctrine, and because of their acceptance of it, they have received a false god in their lives. Because of this, they cannot retain the knowledge of words of the true God. The Bible says it like this, in Romans:

And even as they did not like to retain God in their knowledge, God gave them over to a reprobate mind, to do those things which are not convenient.

Romans 1:28

God is saying that because they chose to embrace the false god teachings, He gave them over to them and their minds now belong to the replacement god doctrine that they have received. When you listen to music and embrace false teachings in your music, you are accepting another god, and the true and living God is no longer your god. He will not be a god to you, but He must be the only God to you! Consequently, it's even hard to concentrate and pray when you are listening to hip-hop and other forms of secular music that have this hidden agenda. Your prayer life dies because essentially, you have another god that your life is being governed by or that is ministering to you, instead of the Holy Spirit. Therefore, when you try to pray to the true and living God, your mind wanders, and you cannot stay focused. Ever wonder why sometimes you're trying to talk with God, but your mind is thinking about other things? Why does this happen? Because there is a false god doctrine in your life, and the true and living God will not tolerate the existence or acceptance of any other god, in word, deed, or song. Here is what He said to Israel about it:

And in all things that I have said unto you be circumspect: and make no mention of the name of other gods, neither let it be heard out of thy mouth.

Exodus 23:13 KJV

Chapter 14

Unbelief

I remember encountering the spirit of hip-hop in a guy named Howard once. He began to tell us that he felt something in the pit of his stomach. Well, when I began to pray and address the issue, a demon inside of him manifested. It overtook his character and his very demeanor. Howard was a soft-spoken, very quiet person, but when this spirit manifested in him, he became obnoxious and bold. It changed his face and his posture. He began jeering at me and talking plenty of trash. I asked the spirit who it was, and he said, "Unbelief!" and began snarling at me. He proceeded to tell me how much he hated me and wanted to kill me. But, of course, that made me rejoice. I do not want a demon to ever get comfortable around me. But anyway, this spirit overtook Howard and began to tell us his purpose. The spirit said that Howard did not believe in the gifts of God and what he saw happening in church. The demon said that Howard began to search for too much informational proof about the workings of the Spirit of God. The demon told us that he did not believe in things that were unseen and he doubted God's power in his heart. The spirit also said that Howard turned to hip-hop as a source of information and learning. The evil spirit even bragged about the demon spirit of hip-hop being inside of Howard. "Hip-hop is here!" shouted the demon, and it began to brag about the presence of that spirit inside of this young man.

In Jesus' name, I rebuked Unbelief and demanded that hip-hop surface. I wish you could have seen the total change in this young man's body when hip-hop manifested in him. He folded up and jumped up into the windowsill, as if he were preparing to jump out of the window! I commanded hip-hop not do that, and the spirit subsided, but he stayed seated where he was, hissing at me. The demon then said very loudly, "We hate you!" I asked, "Why?" The spirit said, "Because you know about us. You know what we are up to. Our exploitation is not secret to you!" In the power of Jesus' name, I cast hip-hop out with very little resistance, perhaps because the Lord has had me deal with it so many times before.

After that, Howard sat down, and Unbelief came back. Howard sat and began to brag and be very arrogant, thinking that he was something with this spirit controlling his body. After addressing this spirit for a while, I knew that God had appointed this time, and the demon was going to be cast it out. The spirit said, "Not without a fight!" I remember telling the spirit that there would be no fight, and that it was about to be manhandled by us. (Again, this was in the early days when we were still learning about demons and deliverance. I had a huge friend named Andre there with me, and he was ready to hold him down while we dealt with him.) But the spirit of God spoke to me and said, "DO NOT TOUCH HIM; LET THE ANGELS DO IT!" I was thinking, *Lord, this guy is going to tear this place up if we do not contain him.* But God spoke ever so clearly to me, and I told the others who were with me not to touch him, that the angels were going to restrain him. They all looked surprised as well because the spirit in Howard kept talking about how he was going to tear the place up before it came out. Well, I proceeded to cast the demon of Unbelief out of Howard, and at the moment that we commanded the spirit to come out, Howard, controlled by his demon, jumped up in the air, ready to run. I yelled to the others with me, "Do not touch him," and then I commanded the angels of God to grab him. Howard then froze in mid-thrust and strained to get loose, but could not. The angels were holding him up and would not let him go. He struggled and struggled and could not get loose. I then commanded the angels to force him down to the ground, and as he struggled, his knees buckled, and he fell to his knees. I was then led to say to the angels, "Put him on the ground," and the angels of God slammed him down flat on his face. Now, this next part is very unbelievable (really all of it, if you are an unbeliever), but I had several witnesses who saw this with me. The Lord told me to tell the angels to flip him over on his back so I could deal with Unbelief, and Howard came up off the ground and flipped over as if he levitated! The angels of God actually picked him up and flipped him over on his back. I then began to minister to him, and the demon was loosed from him. He was totally set free by the power of God!

God later began to deal with me about the spirit of Unbelief. Unbelief drives hip-hop. Because hip-hop is a false religion, it has to be accepted through a person's unbelief in the true and living God. You cannot believe in the power of God and the power of hip-hop because hip-hop is a substitute for the truth. Howard told us later that he could not even listen to many Christian rappers after his deliverance because it messed with his spirit and started bringing old feelings of unbelief back. Why? Because many holy hip-hoppers are bound by the same spirit of Unbelief that was in Howard. It's this spirit that says that the power of God and the gifts of the Holy Spirit of God are not operational in modern-day believers. It's this spirit that says, in order to draw the youth, we must subscribe to hip-hop and be like them instead of allowing them to be supernaturally drawn by the Spirit of God through the gifts of God in operation. Fundamentalists are really unbelievers. Sure, they believe in the Bible and Jesus, but they deny the gifts of God in operation. They are unbelieving believers. They deny the filling of the Holy Ghost and the power of God speaking through, working through, and using modern-day believers to cast out devils, heal the sick, and raise the dead. This is the spirit that we cast out of Howard and that is in operation in many so-called believers today. The Bible says:

> And these signs shall follow them that believe; in my name shall they cast out devils; they shall speak with new tongues; they shall take up serpents; and if they drink any deadly thing, it shall not hurt them; they shall lay hands on the sick, and they shall recover.
>
> Mark 16:17-18 KJV

When you do not believe in the signs following, then you do not believe in the truth of the Word, and you have a form of godliness, but deny the power! (2 Timothy 3:5). How can you cast out a demon, heal the sick, or do anything that Jesus and the apostles did, and God's Spirit is currently doing, if you do not believe the gifts are still in operation? As a result of your unbelief, you are limited to gimmicks, natural methods, and cunning resources to reach this world. You have to rely on your own ability and your knowledge. You are learning much, rather than trusting the Spirit of God and the indwelling of the Holy Ghost to empower you to do things for the kingdom of God. This is why Howard and many others sought hip-hop out. They are on a quest to find knowledge and power because they do not believe in the works they have seen God perform. And this is why holy hip-hop is so dangerous, because it uses the same principle of using a man-made method to reach the youth, instead of the power of God being utilized as the source of conviction unto repentance. Hip-hop is a demon spirit, and I have cast this spirit out of many young people. But it almost always is attached to some form of unbelief that resides in the heart of its victims. And its entry point can be from a variety of sources.

Someone could have told a victim that he or she loved the person, and then abused that person, thus, he or she stopped believing in love. Someone could have pretended to be a strong Christian, but behind closed doors, violated that person in some way, thus he or she stopped believing in God's power. Someone could have said something or done something to that person in church that was inconsistent and made him or her feel inferior or hurt, and that caused the person to stop believing in church. Someone could have gotten sick or died who was very close to that person, and though he or she prayed for healing, it did not happen. That person stopped believing in the gifts of God. These things must be dealt with in a believer, and forgiveness must take place. Hip-hop only comes to strengthen the disbelief and give them another source of rebellion and self-affirming power to rise above the hurt and forsake the source of the hurt. But this is not God's way of dealing with unforgiveness. You do not build up walls of rebellion and solitude, but you forgive the person who hurt you. Hip-hop validates hate and works against God's healing of a person who has been subjected to these situations.

The Bible says:

For our struggle is not against flesh and blood, but against the rulers, against the powers, against the world forces of this darkness, against the spiritual forces of wickedness in the heavenly places.

Ephesians 6:12 NASB

This makes it possible for us to forgive anyone of anything. Why? Because we know that flesh-and-blood people are not our enemies. I mentioned earlier my own issues I had to overcome with being sexually abused by women in my church. I believe that the enemy purposely did this because he knew one day I would be working in the church. He thought that by causing these "churchgoing" women to molest and abuse me, I would no longer trust people in the church. I believe this is why the enemy seeks to use ministers and priests to molest children, and then exposes their sins to the world through the media. This way, he can discredit the church and cause people not to trust God's servants. For a season, the devil's plan worked in my life. I did not trust anyone in the church! I thought everyone in the church was phony. I vowed never to set foot in church again. But later, I realized that it was all the plan of the enemy. It's just a shame that the enemy can use "church folks" to get his plan accomplished. When we, as believers, are sinning or doing things that are not godly, chances are we are hurting someone and causing young Christians to stumble. We must be careful that we are not working for the enemy while we are trying to live for God. I am sure those women who molested me never thought that they were working for the enemy. I am sure they were just acting out some of the horrible things that were done to them in their childhood. Nevertheless, we must not allow the enemy to use us like that. We must choose whose side we are on. Jesus said that we are either for Him or against Him. Either we are gathering, or scattering abroad! Matthew 12:30 says, "He that is not with me is against me; and he that gathereth not with me scattereth abroad."

Forgiving and Being Forgiven

For years, I blamed my womanizing and sexual addiction on those women. When God spoke to me and told me to forgive those who had hurt me, I did not want to do it. I felt like they did me wrong and ruined who I was. I felt like they stole my innocence and caused me to be a sex addict. "It's their fault I'm addicted to sex," I told the Lord. Then God showed me myself and let me see all the girls I was hurting through my sexual promiscuity. He showed me that I needed their forgiveness because I was lying and cheating on them to get what I wanted, and that made me no different from the women that violated me. We all needed His forgiveness, and all I could do was cry and repent for what I was doing and forgive those who hurt me. We must never forget that we will need the grace of God and His forgiveness for our sins as well as to forgive others for their sins. Jesus prayed this prayer and said, "And forgive us our sins; for we also forgive every one that is indebted to us" (Luke 11:4).

If you are reading this book and have been hurt by anyone, especially someone in the church, the only way you can progress is to first forgive that person. This is the only way you can stop the plan of Satan in your life. Satan knows that the Bible says in Matthew 18:35, unless you forgive your brother his sins against you, your heavenly Father will not forgive your sins against Him.

So what the devil does is use people to offend you. In most cases, instead of us recognizing that an evil spirit is using the person, we begin to hate that person. This locks up our fellowship with God because He will not forgive us unless we forgive others. Consequently, many Christians can never move past this point. Thus, the devil's plan to stop God's purpose in your life is successful until you forgive all who have hurt you. This is why Jesus prayed as He was being crucified on the cross, "Father, forgive them; for they know not what they do" (Luke 23:34). Jesus knew that they were only being controlled by the powers of darkness.

Remember, Satan can use any non-Christian or any weak Christian to accomplish his plan in your life. Unforgiveness can many times birth the same sin in your heart. I run across thousands of young boys who hate their fathers because they were deadbeats and did not take care of them. It is very difficult for a young boy to watch his father mistreat his mother as well as reject him. However, in almost every case, that young, hurt, angry boy is on his way to becoming just like his father was. That unforgiveness is buried deep inside of his spirit and causes him to not hear or see the truth. Thus, he begins to follow the same pattern his father followed at his age— carelessly sleeping with woman and making babies he cannot take care of with women he does not even desire to wed. This cycle starts in our youth and is usually centered on some form of unforgiveness. In addition, it begins to bring your purpose and God's desire for you to a screeching halt. This is why you cannot go forward until you forgive, from the heart, everyone who ever hurt you. Many of our prayers are not being answered today because of unforgiveness. I used to get so tired of saying, "It must not have been God's will," after my prayers seemed never to get answered. But one day, I read where Jesus said, when you stand praying, FORGIVE so that your prayers will be answered.

> And when ye stand praying, forgive, if ye have ought against any: that your Father also which is in heaven may forgive you your trespasses.
>
> Mark 11:25

God was not even hearing my prayers because of my unforgiveness toward those who abused me. I had to first give that to God and forgive them. After that, God began to speak to me and answer my prayers. Unforgiveness also opens the door to spiritual torment. Matthew 18:34 says, "And his lord was wroth, and *delivered him to the tormentors*, till he should pay all that was due unto him" (emphasis added).

"The tormentors" in this verse refers to the spiritual torment of demons that have a legal right to attack you because of your unforgiveness. Unforgiveness opens the door to torment from doubt and unbelief, as we stop trusting in God's ability to distribute mercy and justice.

Before we go any further, you may be struggling with the sin of unforgiveness, and we need to take this time and deal with that. I want to lead you in a prayer of forgiveness toward everyone who has ever offended, abused, molested, neglected, or mistreated you. Forgiving someone does not mean that you deny what happened, but it does mean that you let them "off the hook," and they no longer owe you anything. Pray with me.

"Dear heavenly Father, I come needing to be forgiven by You for not forgiving others as I should. At this very moment, there are people in my life I still have not forgiven. But right now, as an act of my will, I forgive (say the person's name) for (say what he or she did). This person no longer owes me anything, and Lord, I ask that You forgive this person also. I recognize that this person was only being used of the devil.

"Now I command all evil spirits associated with my unforgiveness and unbelief to leave me right now, in Jesus' name."

Chapter 15

But He Has a Chainsaw!

Ever have a beer commercial sober you up? I am referring to a funny beer commercial I saw that had a very good point. Now, I am not into the whole "sippin' saint" thing. I'm not endorsing beer or drinking alcohol at all, but this funny commercial makes a good point. The commercial was about a man and a woman driving at night, lost, trying to get to their destination. As they are driving, they spot a very dangerous-looking hitchhiker, who had a case of beer in one hand and an old rusty ax in the other hand. The guy who is driving wanted to stop and pick up the hitchhiker because he had his favorite beer, but the lady kept saying, "But he has an ax!" He kept insisting, "But he has my favorite beer, and besides, there's probably a reason for the ax. Let's ask him." Before they pick him up, they ask him, "What's the ax for?" And this gruesome and scary-looking man says in a deep voice, "Oh, it's a bottle opener!" Blinded by his desire for the beer, his better judgment gets thrown out, and though this guy has a tool for destruction in his hand, the driver says to him, "Good, hop on in." So because of the driver's desire for his favorite beer, they pick him up, and "ax man" gets in their backseat!

After they are driving awhile, the driver sees another hitchhiker, and this guy is even creepier than the first hitchhiker. This huge man is wearing a ski mask and also is holding the driver's favorite beer in one hand, but this guy has a chainsaw in the other hand! The driver says, "Hey, look, he has my favorite beer; let's pick him up," and ax man sheepishly says from the backseat, "But, he has a chainsaw!" That commercial had me cracking up, but then the reality of it hit me, and it wasn't funny anymore. Many pastors, blinded by their desire for money and crowds, are allowing the devil into the back-seat of the church: the choir loft. In one hand, he has entertainment, and in the other hand is a tool for destroying their young people: hip-hop.

There is a new move in our nation called holy hip-hop. It's a knock-off version of true hip-hop, but it is getting very popular among youth pastors and churches that do not know how to reach the youth of their communities effectively. Instead of fasting, praying, and seeking God for His Spirit to draw hearts that truly want to repent, they turn to holy hip-hop, which will speak the language, promote the look and appeal of the subculture, and then add the message of Christ to it. See, holy hip-hoppers believe that they can reach real hip-hoppers by being hip-hoppers—just holy ones. They believe they are an alternative to the real hip-hop, so that when you give your life to Christ, you still can be represented by a holy version of hip-hop. They also believe that hip-hop can be holy because God changed you or me from our sinful state into a holy person.

When I was not in Christ, I was a thief and a crook. Now that I am saved, am I a holy crook? I guess next the gothic culture is going to have a bootleg, holy version of the real thing eventually (as crazy as it seems, someone may already be doing this). Can't you just see the kids in your youth group wearing black clothing and nail polish, with tattoos and piercings everywhere, and looking like walking dead people? Then the holy gothic recording artist/minister comes in and validates them. He will look like Marilyn Manson, sound like Marilyn Manson, and dress like Marilyn Manson, but he will sing about Christ.

Will this reach the youth? Will these youth be transformed by the power of God and begin to look and act like NEW CREATURES? No, they will continue to live and look like the subculture that had them spiritually bound in the first place. These methods always look good on the surface and can be justified by quoting, "I become all things to all men. . . ." Okay, let's become a part of the pornographic culture to reach the pornographers. This is ridiculous. To reach the gothic subculture or any other subculture, you must ask the real question "Why are they gothic?"

In the case of the creation of the gothic subculture, first, there was heavy metal music. Then those in the occult began to use this particular subculture of the music to push their agenda. The spirit of witchcraft began to be released through the satanic artist who made the music. Understand that when a Satan-worshiping musician plays music, he gives spirits of darkness a vessel to work through. Through an evolution of the genre and the subculture, the gothic spirit manifested, and those who wanted to rebel and be outcasts of their mainstream culture subscribed to it. This formed the subculture of goth! They began to emulate the rebellion and gave the spirit of evil and darkness another place to manifest. Whether you believe it or not, the devil uses music as a vehicle to transfer spirits.

For the intellectual fundamentalists who don't subscribe to evil spirits and the devil, let me ask you, "How is it that you teach that the spirit of God operates through your music, but you don't believe that evil spirits can operate through secular music?" Doesn't the Bible teach the fight that we are fighting isn't flesh and blood?

> For we wrestle not against flesh and blood, but against principalities, against powers, against the rulers of the darkness of this world, against spiritual wickedness in high places.
> Ephesians 6:12

I don't think that any fundamentalists would deny that we are in a spiritual wrestling match, but they want to fight only on the natural level, when the Word of God clearly states that we are in a spiritual battle with spiritual beings. It is remarkable to me that even the secular music industry understands the transfer of spirits in music, while the Christian artist denies that anything like this exists.

Notice the term "spiritual wickedness" in Ephesians 6:12. What would the term "spiritual wickedness" be referring to? Maybe it is referring to the mixing of the sacred with the secular! Could it be referencing holy (spiritual) hip-hop (wickedness)?

The real problem with goth kids is spiritual! If you would deal with the spirit of rebellion in them, they would abandon goth altogether. It is the same with hip-hop! Notice that goth is not a type of music, but it is a way of life. If hip-hop is teaching rebellion and is a spiritual problem, then why join forces with it? Why try to redeem something that was birthed out of lack, poverty, rebellion, and ethnocentricity? Why not allow God to gift you supernaturally to deal with the spirit in the youths that is pulling them to hip-hop in the first place? I would not allow a person that is pierced all up, tattooed all over, and dressed in black with dark makeup and a scary countenance to get up before my youths and teach them anything. They are representing rebellion, and they are validating rebellion in the lives of the youth.

Well, I also refuse to allow a man who looks thugged-out or gangstered-up, or a girl who is dressed "hoochie-fied" and whorish to get up and validate the hip-hop lifestyle in my church. Many of our youths cannot get decent jobs or even finish school because they refuse to change their look for our society. They want to look gang-stered-up and thugged-out like the hip-hop artists they see, but those artists are paid for looking like that, and our kids can't get ahead looking like them.

And now, there are Christian versions of these thugs and gang-sters. They want to come to your church, dressed like a hoodlum, and get up before your youth to preach and rap? They want to give props to hip-hop and bring this foul belief system into your church to vali-date the rebellion that already exists among your youth. They want to show your young boys that wearing big diamond earrings, doo-rags, and baseball caps over wave caps is okay for church service.

Did you ever notice that the holy hip-hoppers always give "props" to hip-hop, not holy hip-hop? Even at some of their concerts, they have the youth chanting, "Hip-hop! Hip-hop!" not, "Holy hip-hop! Holy hip-hop!" I guess holy hip-hop has too many syllables. I ask you, "Is it holy for the holy hip-hoppers to show your young boys to throw up gang signs and pull up their pants all day because they are sagging so low? Do we believe that the established church should not have anything to say about this?" Even public schools know that they cannot allow the subculture of hip-hop to take over and maintain order in an institution of learning. Every school district I know of has rules against the many elements of hip-hop. They won't allow the music, the bandannas, the sagging, the "hoochie-mama" outfits, doo-rags, jerseys, or hats. So is the church supposed to have lower standards than public schools? I thought we were the salt of the earth and the light of the world. Wake up, people! Goth people are probably saying, "But hip-hop has a chainsaw!"

Can't you see what's going on? If hip-hop was birthed through poverty, idolatry, and ignorance, then why is it being used by Christians to reach youths? Shouldn't we reach out to them with an example of how the power of God changes a person, rather than how your insides can change, but it does not affect the outside? A gang member wears a rag to symbolize where he belongs. A prisoner wears his pants sagging to show that he has no belt or that he is a homosexual lover to someone. A prostitute dresses revealingly and in tight clothes to show that she is a whore and will sell you some. If God wants to change them, will He use their own kind to reach them?

I mean, would He use a holy gang member? Would He use a saved thug? Would He use a woman who dresses like a whore to reach a prostitute? This does not make sense. Where is the change? Wouldn't it be more effective to have a person who once dressed like a whore, a gang member, or a prisoner to show the change that God made to his or her appearance by him or her changing first? Let's get real. I guess so many of our churches are so desperate for the attention of their youth that they will allow a gospel gangster, a holy hoodlum, or even a preachin' pimp to come and give their youth some tight beats and rhymes.

But the wise man wins the soul, right? NO! Proverbs 11:30 says, "He that winneth souls is wise" (KJV). There is a big difference between that question and this Scripture. This Scripture is not saying that we should be wise and cleaver in coming up with ways to attract people to God. It's basically stating a fact. If you win souls, you are wise. If you obey God, walk in His way, and allow His Spirit to operate through you, you will win souls, and thus, you are wise. But we tend to make the Scripture mean that if we think up ways to reach people and use craftiness in doing it, then we are wise! The Bible is clear in 2 Corinthians 4 about using craftiness and handling the Word of God deceitfully.

But have renounced the hidden things of dishonesty, not walking in craftiness, nor handling the word of God deceitfully; but by manifestation of the truth commending ourselves to every man's conscience in the sight of God.

2 Corinthians 4:2

We cannot pretend we're one thing to get people's attention, and then show them that we are another thing. In other words, you can't use the actual music of the "real" hip-hop and the religion of hip-hop to get the youths' attention so you can minister to them. The only reason they are drawn to this subculture in the first place is because of its supernatural pull and how it agrees with their lifestyle. If there is such a thing as holy hip-hop, then why is the world's version just plain hip-hop? Why don't they call what they are doing secular hip-hop or gangster hip-hop? To them, it's just hip-hop because they are the original. But the church has the counterfeit and has to change the definition of the word to be a part of it. The name suggests that to make it holy is to make it non-authentic or to make it something that it is not. This is because hip-hop was created for the world. For someone in the church to amend it and add the prefix "holy" to it suggests that it's not original and is a knock-off version of what it was created to be. Sure, God made everything, and He made music. He is the Creator, but we are manufacturers. We take the talent, material, and elements that God gave us, and we manufacture from His creations. There was no hip-hop in the Garden of Eden, but there were raw materials that man could use to create it. Many holy hip-hoppers try to use the following Scripture to justify using hip-hop:

For by him were all things created, that are in heaven, and that are in earth, visible and invisible, whether they be thrones, or dominions, or principalities, or powers: all things were created by him, and for him.

Colossians 1:16

It must be understood that just because something is in existence does not mean that God created it and sanctions it. Child pornography exists, yet God didn't create it, nor does He use it in any way. When we talk about music and subculture, we are talking about something that was manufactured using the raw materials and talents that God created. So, in that sense, sure, God created everything. But many things that are manufactured by man God does not want credited back to Him.

I know you are probably asking yourself, "Why don't they just call it Christian rap and leave out the hip-hop part? The answer: Because they can't. Christian rap does not mimic the secular industry enough for them. Now, if you are going to be a Christian version of the Wu-Tang Clan, then you have to effectively mimic the group. You can't just rap and make beats, but you have to dress like the group's members, move around on stage like them, and look like them. This is where hip-hop comes in. Hip-hop keeps the looks, the flare, and the flavor in the performance so that they can effectively emulate the secular version of themselves.

When a Christian rap group does not want to be associated with hip-hop in any way, then the group's members don't emulate secular artists. They can have their own style, their own flavor, and their own God-given creativity, and not depend on hip-hop to dictate to them what they should be like. Hip-hop is the spirit that brings authenticity to holy hip-hoppers. Without it, they can't be like their worldly heroes of hip-hop. They will have to give credit to God alone and can no longer pay tribute to hip-hop. Thus, it puts them out of the loop, and they must stand on their own. They cannot sell a lot of CDs; they won't get the Dove Award. They won't stand out without hip-hop because the people they say they are reaching will only respect their God if hip-hop is used to bring Him to them. In many of their raps, they make hip-hop equal to God and make hip-hop and the gospel a "team." Since when did hip-hop become equal with the gospel of Jesus Christ? Hip-hop denounces Christ! But I guess when you call it "holy hip-hop," Christ can be equal to hip-hop, and they can work together to reach the world like Kanye West states in his blockbuster hit song "Jesus Walks."

Why call it holy hip-hop and not believe in the gifts of the Holy Ghost? The Holy Ghost will draw the sinner, but many holy hip-hop rappers deny the gifts and do not deal with the spirit realm concerning hip-hop and the world. They don't cast out demons, they don't believe in divine healing, and many don't even believe in the baptism of the Holy Ghost! So what do they leave the youth with that they are trying to reach? Beats, rhymes, and positive lyrics, rather than negative ones. They are an alternative, with no authenticity. Sure, the kids are drawn by the beats and the hip-hop because that's where they are. Kanye West is packing out church altars when he makes his appeal for salvation, even though his music promotes sin, sex, and violence. How is he any different from a holy hip-hopper? They are both using hip-hop to reach the youth, right? His is positive, right? The one thing I can appreciate about Kanye West is that he is true to what he does. He is not trying to change hip-hop into something holy. He knows that it's all just hip-hop! Only the church is foolish enough to bring this demonic subculture in and call it just music. Real hip-hoppers know that music has little to do with it. It's the enemy's agenda. Even KRS ONE knew that the only way to get the knowledge of self and his "Black man is god" teachings into the church was to use holy hip-hop! He was one of the founding fathers of hip-hop, so he is an advocate of holy hip-hop and any other form of worship through hip-hop. He says that all religions can worship through hip-hop because hip-hop is like Christ! To real hip-hoppers, it's Christlike because to them, no man cometh to the Father but through a mixture of their beliefs and hip-hop! Even Da'T.R.U.T.H., a knockoff gospel version of Jay-Z, said in his CD, "Hip-hop and the gospel, what a dynamic team!" Does the gospel need hip-hop?

These same artists will be the first to deny that the gifts of God are in operation in the church. They can't understand the spirit behind hip-hop because they don't even have faith in the Holy Spirit behind the gifts of God! But what about the kids who are possessed by demons, bound by spiritual issues, or sick and need to be healed? Can a fundamentalist rapper who denies the very power of the Holy Ghost be effective in this situation? Giving them beats and rhymes will not do it.

No More Gimmicks!

Effective youth ministries don't need gimmicks. Youth pastors and youth ministers, wake up! If you need hip-hop to reach your youth, then you are not an effective youth minister! If you need to give the youth what they want instead of what they need, then you are no better than an irresponsible parent who spoils his child. If you have to keep having hip-hop lock-ins, concerts, praise dance festivals, field trips, food, and candy to keep your youth interested in your youth ministry, then you need to reevaluate whether or not God has truly called you to be a youth minister. Maybe you missed your call of being an amusement park attendant or a babysitter. A truly effective youth minister can preach the Word of God and cause the youths to go out and win other youths. When a youth ministry is really effective, they are able to grow based on the Word of God being preached, and not on gimmicks, fun times, or music. Youths desire the supernatural power of God just like adults. But when you have a carnal youth leader who cannot manifest the power of God and deal with demons, spirits, and witchcraft, then the youths will need fun and activities to stay interested. If you are not able to give them a true move of God in your youth ministry, then you have to compete with the world! You will have to give them what the world is giving them. If there are parties and dances happening at their schools, you will have to have one the same night, but stamp Jesus on it. If there are concerts and hip-hop clubs happening around you, you will have to have concerts and clubs with a Jesus stamp. You will always be led by the world and in direct competition with the world. Hip-hop will become your nemesis, and rather than beating it by the power of the Holy Ghost, transforming, and moving through your youth ministry, you will have to join it because it's easier than seeking a real move of God. The beats will take the place of the Spirit of God. The holy hip-hoppers will come in and promote themselves by looking the part, acting the part, and promoting the real hip-hoppers that they stole their style from. Then the kids will yell and scream and come to the altar because of the beats. But they will leave the service, only to listen to the real hip-hop in their cars or at home. And as long as they continue to listen to the real hip-hoppers and secular artists, the holy hip-hop will be a fill-in for them. Since they can't have Usher and Lil Jon in the church, then they will take the Cross Movement or Lil iROCC for now. You better believe when they get home, they will desire the real deal. Do not get me wrong; if it is Christian rap or Gospel rap, then it does not compare itself with the world's artists because there is no hip-hop subculture involved with it. If a person considers himself a holy hip-hopper or says he is using hip-hop, then he is comparing himself to something that is in the world.

Holy hip-hoppers are not the real thing and will only make the real hip-hop more powerful. This makes KRS ONE's prophecy about hip-hop true because he stated that all religions could worship through hip-hop! He believes that the religion of hip-hop and the belief in the Black man being god are essential in worshiping the true God of this planet. He says that hip-hop must be reckoned with by all people of color and must be used by every religion to effectively reach our people. This is putting hip-hop equal with God and saying that in order to get to God, you must use hip-hop! He even came out with a holy hip-hop CD to preach this doctrine and used holy hip-hoppers T-Bone and BB Jay on it for validation! So it appears that the holy hip-hop movement is fulfilling the prophecy of hip-hop's founders by making it a necessary tool for effective ministry. The only tool necessary for effective ministry, however, is the preaching of the gospel and the drawing of the Holy Ghost. I know this may sound foolish to many, but it is called "foolishness of preaching."

> For after that in the wisdom of God the world by wisdom knew not God, it pleased God by the foolishness of preaching to save them that believe.
>
> 1 Corinthians 1:21 KJV

We have thousands of saved and hip-hop-free teenagers who will attest to this truth.

Chapter 16

Holy Hip-hop?

Only uninformed church folks consider hip-hop a music style or genre. But to its creators and any real hip-hopper, it is considered a religion, a belief system, a subculture, or a "way of life." P. Diddy stated on a talk show, when asked what the difference between hip-hop and rap was, "Rap is the music, but hip-hop is my life. . . . As a matter of fact, hip-hop is life!" Christians only call hip-hop a music form in efforts to get it accepted in the church and the lives of believers.

This mask is what the enemy is using to deceive the church into embracing this religion and get it in the lives of our youths and accepted by the leadership of the church. Hip-hop was founded in the streets as a voice for the people who felt they had no voice. But when Christ comes in the picture, He becomes the voice, yet holy hip-hoppers still want to hang on to the streets and the street behavior because they feel it legitimizes them and their efforts to prosper off of the church. Many of their songs are still gangster-oriented and thug-promoting, and carry the street mentality, which only further promotes the agenda of the hip-hopper in its original form. Saying hip-hop is holy is like saying whatever you were before Christ is still who you are, just with salvation. Only a fundamentalist believer could buy into this. Anyone who is born of God and filled with the Holy Ghost knows that "if any man be in Christ, he is a new creature!" Old things are past away. The old behaviors that reflected your negative upbringing are behind you, and you begin to walk in the newness of life. The old gang-related attire is thrown away, and now you dress differently. The old gang signs and vulgar language you spoke is changed to a new way of talking. You don't continue to mimic the demonic lifestyle you once lived when you were in the streets, but you begin to grow and change. And it's this change that occurs when you are filled with the Spirit of God. So why are holy hip-hoppers continually promoting the streets to reach the streets? Why don't they show the real hip-hoppers that God can produce change in you? Why don't they show progress and promote the fact that they are no longer hip-hoppers, but they are believers who are set apart and conformed into the image of Christ? When God saved Saul on the road to Damascus, He did not make Paul a holy Pharisee! Paul left that religious subculture and became a believer. He preached to the Pharisees not as a Pharisee, but as a believer, and thus, many were converted. It took God taking him out, teaching and preparing him for fourteen years, and removing the Pharisee "way of life" from him to make him effective. It's when people see the change in others that they see that change is possible for them. But when we try to reach them by becoming like them, we forfeit the very ability to show them that change is possible.

People of God, understand that holy hip-hop is a ridiculous push to make money from the real hip-hop! It's a subculture of a subculture, and God does not need it. If you must use your ideas to reach youth, then you don't have the power of God operating through you. Anyone can make beats and rhymes and attract youth. Kanye West is doing a good job of having altar calls and using hip-hop to preach his messages. What's the difference between Kanye West and a holy hip-hopper? If beats and rhymes are needed to reach the youth, then stop bringing these "posers" and "wanna-be" holy hip-hoppers to your churches, and get the real thing. Get Kanye West and DMX to come and draw a crowd at the altar. They are able to get the youth up front and have altar prayers. They are able to minister Christ to the youth just as effectively as the imitation hip-hoppers (holy hip-hoppers.) Of course, I'm being facetious, but I'm trying to make a point. If hip-hop is to be used, then don't you think God will use the real hip-hoppers, rather than the imitation ones? Hip-hop is of the devil, and holy hip-hop is a joke. God needs holy hip-hoppers as much as He needs Kanye West or DMX. Of course, I'm not saying to get secular folks to minister to God's people. I'm just trying to use an extreme example to make a point. Unfortunately, there is so much mixture in the church and the world, the lines are getting blurred. As a matter of fact, real hip-hoppers are seeking validation from the church, and they are getting it.

Mixture

My God, what's going on? You turn on the award show, and you see the Gospel artist with the secular artist. Why are Gospel artists trying to go back into the world? We turn on BET awards, and we see Kanye West singing with Yolanda Adams like there is nothing wrong with it. She even did a song with Bone Thugs-n-Harmony, one of the most demonic groups ever! What is going on? Why are all the sex-cussing secular artists recording with the Gospel folks? The Lord said, "It's happened before."

You see, in the Acts chapter 16, there's a story of a lady who walked through a town, and she was a slave, but she practiced witchcraft. She made her masters a lot of money by telling people's fortunes. But there was a brand new market growing in that city that she hadn't tapped into yet. And that was the Christian market. There was a man walking through the city named Paul. He wasn't just any man; he was a man of God. She began to declare that Paul was a man of the Most High God. She kept saying, "These are the men of the Most High God." And she was telling the truth. So most of us looking at this story say, "What's wrong with that?" But Paul turned around and rebuked her. The reason Paul rebuked her, though she was telling the truth, is because she was really trying to get another market. You see, she couldn't get the Christians to do what she wanted because they didn't know if she could do what she was saying. *So,* she thought, *if I can go behind the man of God and begin to show that I'm with the man of God, then I'll gain credibility with the folks who weren't with me before. And once they hear me say the truth about the man of God, then they will say, "Hey, she really does know what she is talking about. Please, tell me my future."* So what she was really doing was using Paul as an enabler.

Listen, what these secular artists are doing is trying to gain a new market. You see, Christians wouldn't have known much about India Arie until she stepped on the stage at T.D. Jakes' demonic Christian gathering called MegaFest. Kanye West wouldn't have been able to perform at church had he not been validated by Ebenezer Baptist Church in Maryland, which had him come minister to its youth. Most church folks wouldn't have known about him if he hadn't performed at the awards with Yolanda Adams. You see, they need enablers to put them in the church. Now, I know I'm messing with your music. I'm sure many of you are thinking, *I thought this book was against hip-hop? You're in my Gospel record collection now.* I'm sorry, but I must say something because we are losing power, because hip-hop is attempting to turn the Temple of God into the Temple of Doom by using Christian enablers.

Now, if these artists only promoted themselves as entertainers, they might be able to get away with some of there antics, but they claim to be ministers and preachers of the gospel. Yet, if they can't cast out devils and do what the apostles did, then what good are they? Many may argue with the validity of this Scripture, but read what the Bible says in Mark 16:17, 20:

> And these signs shall follow them that believe; in my name shall they cast out devils. . . . And they went forth, and preached every where, the Lord working with them, and confirming the word with signs following.

It's not enough to reach the youth and get their attention with your beats and rhymes. It's not enough, as the Cross Movement says, to "make hip-hop and the gospel a team." Music was never used in the Bible to win souls or reach people for God. It was always the truth of the Word being preached that brought men to repentance. Moreover, for a thugged-out, gangster-looking rapper to stand before your youth and declare he is ministering will only promote the look, the behavior, and the spirit of hip-hop, which we are working so hard to defeat in the body of Christ. We don't need our boys looking like thugs. We don't need our girls dressing like whores. We don't need holy hip-hoppers promoting the beats of the world, the clothing lines of these godless rappers, or the spirit of rebellion and deception.

Okay, let's look at an obvious contradiction of holy hip-hop. Many holy hip-hoppers wear the clothes of artists who publicly oppose God. For instance, if a holy hip-hopper wears Rocawear, he is promoting Jay-Z, who has a back mastered song on an underground album that says "murder, murder, Jesus." Now, why would any Christian want to wear anything that promotes someone who claims he is "Jay-hova" and openly mocks Jesus? And most holy hip-hoppers proudly proclaim that they listen to and are fans of secular hip-hop groups and performers. They give props to them and endorse them in secret, yet try to be the alternative to them in public. This is where they get the flavor and relevance. To properly mock them and sound like them, they have to study them, right?

We need some youth pastors and youth ministers who can minister the Word of God so effectively that the gifts of the Spirit of God will draw the youth and change their hearts. This will cause them to pull the gang gear off and dress like they should so they can go into any cultural circle and prosper. This will cause them to put off the former man and allow God to create a new identity in them so they can show the world the power of God has changed them. This will keep them from being pulled back into the world, because they are trying so hard to fit in with the world to make the world comfortable, rather than being a new creature and reaching men by their example of change.

Would a crack addict want another crack addict ministering to him? Would it be effective to use the crack lifestyle to minister because it speaks the language? To effectively minister to a crack-head, you need to exemplify the change by walking it and showing it. The crack addict has a spiritual problem and needs the Spirit of God to change him. Sure, you can get the person's attention by pretending to be a crack addict, but will that help? Shouldn't you be redeemed and looking like you are no longer a crack addict? The power is not in your relating to the person by your appearance, but the power is in your testimony of change and the visible proof of the change! Didn't those that Jesus changed go and testify of it and show the proof of it? That's how you overcome—not by showing people that you can be a holy crack addict and still walk like, look like, and act like them, but now you are holy with it. The same applies to the holy hip-hop religion/subculture. Coming out of it is the key—not changing it so that you can keep your fix.

The truth makes you free—not music, not a song, not beats! It's the truth! Love tells the truth! Why are we using gimmicks to reach the youths? Why can't we preach an effective word of truth to them without using a subculture that is their stronghold in the first place? It's like we are using the very thing that was a struggle for them to reach them. Don't you know that if the music is their problem, then the music cannot be their answer? That will continue to lead them back to music instead of Christ, and then they won't be able to hear unless music is involved.

If hip-hop can be holy, then why don't the holy hip-hoppers refer to it as holy hip-hop in their songs? For example, Da' T.R.U.T.H. says in one of his songs that "Hip-hop and the gospel, a dynamic team!" Now we know if they are on the same team, that would make them similar. The Word tells us, "How can two walk together, unless they agree?" And it also says, "How can bitter and sweet come from the same fountain?" So obviously, he is referring to holy hip-hop in this statement. But it is clear that he did not call it that. If it is holy hip-hop that he is doing, then why not just say that? Also, Phanatic of the Cross Movement gives thanks to hip-hop in his album credits. Let's examine this:

1. If hip-hop is only beats and rap, why would you thank it? You only thank entities or beings, not inanimate things. He might as well have thanked his microphone, wires, keyboard, and beat machine. (It doesn't matter what they say; these holy hip-hoppers know that hip-hop is more than music.)

2. Why didn't he thank holy hip-hop? And why do they make youth chant, "Hip-hop" over and over at their concerts instead of chanting, "Holy hip-hop?" It is very evident that there is a hidden agenda either by the holy hip-hoppers or the real hip-hoppers. Like my grandmother used to say, "SOMEBODY

IS LYING." Either way, hip-hop is definitely not music, so with that said, what are they chanting to?

Are they chanting, "Hip-hop" because it's a way of life? Jesus said He is the way, the truth, and the life!

Are they chanting it because it's a worldly culture? God said, "Love not the world, neither the things of the world. If any man loves the world, the love of the father is not in him!" Surely, the Cross Movement and others love the Father in the sense that God is their ultimate Leader. However, if they embrace the subculture that does not love God, if they embrace a way of life that does not recognize His Son as the Christ, if they pull the youth of the kingdom out of freedom and back into the bondage of a belief system that serves itself, then they are no different from a secular artist who denies righteous living and preaches Jesus! Read this Scripture:

O foolish Galatians, who hath bewitched you, that ye should not obey the truth, before whose eyes Jesus Christ hath been evidently set forth, crucified among you? This only would I learn of you, Received ye the Spirit by the works of the law, or by the hearing of faith? Are ye so foolish? having begun in the Spirit, are ye now made perfect by the flesh?

Galatians 3:1-3

In other words, is it the Spirit that saves us, or is it something that we do in the flesh, like HIP-HOP that does it? When Christians violate this principle, it makes way for Kanye West and Destiny's Child, who claim Christ, yet promote the world and worldliness. What is the difference?

You struggle to bring your youths out of the culture and into a new way of governing themselves. Thug-free, gangster-free, hoochie-free, and then holy hip-hoppers invite themselves to your ministry, only to put hip-hop right back into them? They move like a hip-hopper, they dress like a hip-hopper, and they go against the grain of the authority of your house. They make the adult worship look silly and irrelevant to your youth. They make the adult worship service boring by comparison. They have all the same elements of the world, and they awaken the former man's self-glorying. They cause the youths to again desire what they had before they came to Christ. They put hip-hop right back at the forefront of their lifestyle and tell them it's okay to embrace a subculture of our American culture, rather than embracing the counterculture of Christianity. They taunt the suit-wearing preachers and make the normal church service seem ineffective when it comes to youth ministry. The youths cannot relate to the adults, and the adults cannot relate to the children.

Then, chaos is born, and the enemy finds his way in the middle of both groups. The church then becomes a haven of confusion, and the devil can keep the youth chasing the world, and adults staying their distance because they do not "understand" the spirit behind the youth's distance. All the while, the holy hip-hoppers are selling a few (and I mean very few) CDs and getting a little recognition! And every major youth function is turned into a big party, complete with the flavor of the world and the spirit of rebellion. Gang signs go up during concerts; crotch-grabbing knock-off rappers begin to emulate what they saw on BET and MTV while injecting small portions of real hip-hop in their music and their chants. The youth come to the altar because they are drawn to an opportunity to stamp Christ on their lifestyle, rather than Christ calling them out of hip-hop. They are not new creatures, but they are old creatures with an upgrade! They go home and struggle with secular music and Christian music. Demons plague their bedrooms and their alone times because there was no real deliverance offered at the festival they attended. The power of the Holy Ghost is denied by the fundamentalist rappers who entertained your youth, and all they received was a "church" version of the real deal hip-hop they are possessed by. They continue to party and hang with sinners. Their lifestyle is only reflective of Christ when they come together to worship, but even then, they are worshiping through a worldly vice called hip-hop. They are trying to get sweet liquids out of a bitter source. All the while, Afrika Bambaataa, KRS ONE, and the other founding fathers of hip-hop are saying to the church, "Job well done!" Now hip-hop is necessary to get people to God; therefore, it is equal to Christ!

Holy Hip-Hop and Dispensationalism

I guess the scariest part of a holy hip-hopper coming to minister to a youth group is the fundamentalist belief system. Holy hip-hoppers like The Cross Movement and Da' T.R.U.T.H. do not believe in casting out devils, speaking in tongues, or even hearing God speak other than through the Bible!

- ❏ They do not reveal these beliefs to the leadership of the church if they are booked, but they do teach their beliefs in their lyrics (hmm, sounds familiar).
- ❏ They teach that God does not speak to men other than through written words in the Bible (the logos).
- ❏ They teach that the gifts of the Spirit are not relevant to these times, but were only in operation during the New Testament period. Now, isn't this a contradiction?

For example, a pastor of a church has the gifts operating in his ministry, and speaks of God giving him visions, words of knowledge, prophecies, and so on. But at the youth concert or service, these fundamental holy hip-hoppers are hiding a secret. The secret is that they don't believe what the pastor has been preaching! They come in and "tolerate" the teachings of the pastors just to get on the stage of the youth ministry. But what is going on in the spirit realm is a form of godliness, but a denial of the power!

Example two: The Cross Movement years ago told us that they turned Kirk Franklin down when he propositioned them to be a part of his music group because they didn't believe in his mixing of secular and Christian music. They told us that they were totally against it. But a few years later, when they signed a distribution deal to get a greater presence in the music industry, guess who they joined forces with? KIRK FRANKLIN! Did Kirk change? No, but they did.

Example three: Da' T.R.U.T.H. told us that he does not believe in the gifts of the Spirit and definitely does not believe in the programming of TBN because there, they are deceivers of our generation. But when Kirk asked him to be on the very station that he stands against, what did he do? He got on there to promote his brand of hip-hop. Standing on a stage in contradiction, he preached his message, never addressing his beliefs about TBN, the Pentecostal movement, or the programming of TBN. So he promoted the very station and person he is in disagreement with. For what reason? You know. To sell CDs! Why don't these artists stand up for their true beliefs and let these pastors and youth leaders know their stand on the Holy Ghost operating? How can they effectively change the lives of the youths without the power of the Holy Ghost in operation? If they deny the gifts, then what do they have to offer other than fancy words and beats? Pastors, youth leaders, parents, and others, BEWARE and understand that this is not right! If artists don't believe in the gifts of the Holy Spirit, then they should not go perform at churches or line themselves up with people who believe the gifts are in operation! These artists are coming in and changing the very belief system of the youth while defying leadership and having a hidden agenda. This can be very dangerous because it will make the adult worship of that particular church where they are performing look silly and ineffective because these holy hip-hoppers have come in and taken a stand against it in their music. If and when a ministry invites them, then it represents the approval of the leadership; thus, the point is made without discussion. And the end of it will be the youth's confusion and misunderstanding of why these types of groups are invited in when they do not follow the beliefs of the church's ministry. This is confusion and is not of God.

Ministering through music

Everyone is not ready to minister to a crowd of people. Just because you were a worldly hip-hop artist does not make your talent kingdom-transferable. There needs to be a time when you sit and allow God to get the filthy lucre out of you. If you used the stage for evil, then you don't need to change partners on the stage, but you need to get off the stage and allow God to rebuild you. Rap is entertainment, not ministry. Once you no longer desire the stage or to perform, then you are ready to be used by God. As long as the desire is spilling over from what you did in the world, then you have not died to who you were.

Even though there is a level of ministry found in Christian music, it's the beat and the melody that are the draw. So when it's time to draw men to Christ, the music should not be used to do it, but the Spirit of God will do it through an effective preacher. Stop the music, stop the dancing, stop all forms of flesh-satisfying, and give the Word of God. Give it to them pure and filled with the power of the Holy Ghost. Truth will make men free. Sure, Christian entertainment is okay for Christians, but not when it promotes a religion that is against truth.

If you deny the power of God, then you must use a vice or a vehicle to get sinners. It means that you cannot use the gifts you have, but you have to use your talents. When people are drawn by talent, then their emotions are ministered to, not their spirit. The music will prick the soul realm, but not change the heart. That is why the youths in our churches are so perverse and sin sick.

They have the all the same things the world has (dance parties for God, the latest dances to gospel music, hip-hop that is called holy, and the sin of the world). This is because the music is entertainment and not a tool for evangelism. True evangelism does not need music. Music is for helps, not a vehicle for saving souls. If music was intended for "reaching the lost," then why didn't Jesus use it? Why didn't the disciples use it? Why wasn't it named in the fivefold ministry? Why did God purposely omit the mention of it in the structure of the fivefold ministry? The answer: because it is not made for reaching the lost. It is entertainment! Sure, it can set the stage for ministry and usher in God's presence, but when was the last time you felt God's presence with loud beats and rappers looking like thugs and killers, calling what they are doing holy? If it's holy, then why can't His presence be invoked through it? It's because a lot of the holy hip-hoppers talk more about themselves and the power they have than God. They talk about their looks, their abilities, and their style when they should be talking about the Lord! But this selfishness is what fuels hip-hop, so it has to bleed over into the knockoff version, holy hip-hop, right? These guys are trying to sell CDs. It's time to stop being echoes and start being true voices. Stop being copies, and be God's originals. Let's bring the Holy Ghost back and start reaching the youth with the gifts instead of our ideas! Let's stop trying to find a profitable way to reach people and start preaching heaven and hell again. This generation does not need the world wrapped in a different package. They need CHANGE!

If you are a Christian rapper, then be one. But if you are a hip-hopper, then stop trying to stamp Christ on it, and just be what you are! Stop being a knockoff, and get out of the church and live through the subculture/religion of it. You can't take parts of it. We are seeing hundreds of thousands saved each year, and we use no music at all! It's the power of God and influence of peers that will win youths, not music!

Ultimately, I believe that holy hip-hop is a substitute for the Holy Ghost. What holy hip-hopper needs the Holy Ghost? The Bible says that no man comes to Christ unless the Father draws him. But according to one Cross Movement song: *". . . hip-hop's the key it's like some cheese to rats; and they'll come if your beats are raw. . . ."*

Obviously, they are depending on the beats to draw men to Christ. Also, there is no need for deliverance with holy hip-hop because you will stay in the same subculture and do basically the same thing you did before; the only difference is that you will do it for Jesus. I can see the day when this line of thinking leads to "holy strip clubs": "I used to strip for the devil; now I strip for Jesus." I might be wrong, but I don't think I have ever heard a holy hip-hopper tell youths to throw away their worldly hip-hop CDs or to pull off their gang paraphernalia. This is what the Holy Ghost would say if He were in charge of these concerts, but since holy hip-hop has been substituted for the Holy Ghost, nothing of this sort would be either said or inferred.

Chapter 17

Reaching Vs. Teaching

There is a difference between Christian rap and holy hip-hop. Christian rap is the music, but holy hip-hop (and all forms of hip-hop) is the lifestyle, or the "way of life," that was created in the street as an outward expression of the rebellion and wrath that existed in the lives of the people who created it. We believe that one of the biggest deceptions of the enemy is to blur the lines of distinction between that which is the art form of rapping and that which is culture or lifestyle-driven. Therefore, we offer this chapter so that those of you who are in the dark when it comes to who or what you are listening to can find clarity in understanding what it is you are embracing as a youth leader, parent, or pastor. If you have standards in your home or your church that you do not want lowered for the sake of entertainment and CD sales, then be careful of what you invite into your house. For example, if you are constantly telling your young boys in your home or ministry, "Pull your pants up," or, "Take off that bandanna or doo-rag in church," then it's important that you stay consistent with your standard and not allow a culture of rappers to come in and go against that standard by dressing in a manner that you feel is not appropriate. We have been called legalistic for this stand, but the bottom line is, whatever the parents or pastors deem appropriate for their ministry should be supported by those who are invited into their ministry. We have spoken to The Cross Movement, Da' T.R.U.T.H., and other holy hip-hoppers that feel these types of regulations are problematic and cause youth to not want to come to church, but we must understand first and foremost, THEY ARE YOUTH! They are not old enough to make those kinds of judgment calls. They have to obey their parents and their leaders. Our high schools and military are fighting hard against this culture to keep a standard of appearance and stop this move of hip-hop to do away with regulating the way a youth dresses or appears, and we feel the church should not give in to it, either. Sure, the holy hip-hoppers can sag their pants, tattoo and pierce themselves all over, wear headgear in church services, slug up their teeth with gold and such, and even throw up gang signs, but what about the youth of your church? Can they get good jobs dressed like a thug? Can they function effectively in a society that considers this attire inappropriate? We were told by the Cross Movement that hip-hop and all its elements are forms of expression to the Black youth. But since when did we start allowing EVERYTHING that we feel to be expressed? There are many things that we feel that should never be expressed. We are not coming against Christian rappers that rap the gospel message of Jesus, but we are coming against those who stamp Jesus on the hip-hop culture. If hip-hop is what they are expressing, then what is their audience receiving, Christ or hip-hop? Why can't they just do Christian rap and not endorse the lifestyle of hip-hop? Why can't they just preach the Word through their music instead of promoting the culture through their actions? Don't be deceived, people of God. This is a dirty trick of the enemy to cause our youths to go after idolatry and self-worship with a little Jesus stamped on it. The holy hip-hoppers are getting their attention, but hip-hop is getting their lifestyles! The holy hip-hoppers are drawing them to the altar, but hip-hop is waiting for them after the show. The spirit of hip-hop is taking over our nation, but the question is, Are you going to stand by and allow it in your home or church youth group?

There is a very powerful way to minister to youths without giving in to this demonic culture. The youths just need the truth of the Word preached to them. I know many holy hip-hoppers say that's not enough, but my Bible says different. People are resorting to this culture as a form of "reaching" this generation because they, themselves, are bound to it! They don't know how to effectively teach the Word and change the lives of their youths, so they resort to hip-hop as a way of keeping their youths interested in the ministry. But the bottom line is, if they were effective, they wouldn't need a culture or lifestyle to preach through, but they could be relevant with the truth. I'm not saying Christian rap music is bad, but I am saying that hip-hop is a move of the enemy. We have cast this demon spirit out of many, and it is now running rampant through churches, youth groups, and youth leaders who want to defend it! Either you are going to use the Holy Ghost or hip-hop! And all across the country, ministries are standing up against hip-hop and choosing the Holy Spirit as the draw for their youth ministries, and the results speak for themselves. Young men who once dressed liked thugs and pimps are now carrying themselves in a way that makes them able to be productive in the workplace, in school, and in church. Young girls who once were bound by indecency and promiscuity from the hip-hop subculture are now behaving like young godly women and dressing appropriately. God is still powerful and does not need the subculture of hip-hop to minister through. We are seeing thousands of youths each weekend get delivered from the hip-hop subculture through our ministry. No entertainment, no culture, no hip-hop, just the truth of the gospel being preached. They denounce the subculture of hip-hop, throw away their ungodly music, and live for God for real! So you really have to ask yourself this: Is hip-hop something they need, or is it just something YOU need?

A very good friend of our ministry's had this to say about it:

For the last ten years, I have served as teacher, youth minister and, more recently, as youth pastor. Throughout my tenure, I have watched, listened to, counseled, and spoken to hundreds of young people. I have always fought against negative trends in African-American culture. Over and over again, I have tried and failed to persuade young people to strive to be more, to do more, and to reach for more without compromising their so-called "blackness." But through that approach, I have always found myself in a constant battle with an unseen foe. Ephesians 6:12 tells us, "Our struggle is not against flesh and blood, but against the rulers, against the authorities, against the powers of this dark world, and against the spiritual forces of evil in the heavenly realm." I have come to the place where I can now see and stand against this principality that has so many young people in bondage. I'm talking about hip-hop. Hip-hop is more than black culture expressing itself; hip-hop is a pervasive spirit that is seeking to kill, steal, and destroy all that it touches. American culture in general has spiraled down into an embarrassing cesspool of lust and greed. America was once heralded as a country founded on morality and Christian values, but now, at any given moment, one can turn on the TV and find an entertainment show highlighting the rise of some porn star into the mainstream. So the reality is that hip-hop only makes up a portion of the demonic attack against America's youth; however, over the last twenty years, it has become the most pervasive enemy of young people. We already know about the misogynistic lyrics of hip-hop and its violent themes, but for African-Americans especially, the spirit of hip-hop has caused the dumbing down of a whole generation.

Hip-hop has created a subculture that has rendered its followers absent from all aspects of society. Youths that follow hip-hop have difficulty functioning at home, in school, at church, and in business. Amongst their peers, these hip-hoppers might be considered in high regard. They are praised as the ones who are "keepin' it real" and "representing the streets." But what happens to hip-hop fans who transition into adulthood unprepared is a tragedy that continues to repeat itself. Far too often, young people find themselves facing the harsh reality that the ideas and values they've rebelled against are now the very ones they must embrace to succeed in life. The principles they once called "corny" are the pillars they need to get a job, live real life, and be successful. The problem is youths don't know how to dress, don't know how to talk, and can't write a resume because of a lack of basic skills and experience. Contrary to popular belief, sitting in a studio all night, making up beats does not make good resume material. If you are like me, you probably have noticed that most conversations with young people are peppered with a whole lot of "Naw mean?" I want to say, "No, I don't know what you mean, and unfortunately, you can't articulate what you mean to me, either." The lifestyle and idol status of hip-hop performers have further helped to destroy our youths' ability to achieve and succeed.

It is about time that our Christian communities stand up and call out this spirit for what it is and what it has done to our youths. Hip-hop has caused the dumbing down of our generation.

The majority of youths who have been steeped in the hip-hop lifestyle are good kids who have grown up listening to hip-hop and living the hip-hop life. They have been slowly lulled to sleep. Most simply need a wake-up call for them to "come out from among them and be separate." They need their leaders and pastors to challenge them to consider the damage that hip-hop has done, particularly in the African-American community, over the last ten years. As Christians, they must be challenged to decide whether the hip-hop subculture is something believers ought to embrace or not. So-called "holy hip-hop" is telling youths it's all right to celebrate the streets, as long as they "do it for Jesus." The message is being preached that it is acceptable to be a gospel gangster and a holy hoodlum. What kind of foolishness is this? We are not gangsters and hoodlums; we are children of the Most High God. We are royalty, new creations in Christ Jesus. We have to warn this next generation about hip-hop's deceptions, or we will be sending them to a hell they will experience in this life and in the one to come. Physical and spiritual hell. Can you imagine in twenty short years an entire segment of our population shut out because they haven't mastered the basics of the English language and basic math and science skills? For many communities, this sad reality is already here. Hip-hop has caused the dumbing down of our generation.

We are long overdue in taking a stand against these negative trends that hip-hop has unleashed on our society. Too many young people can barely read, yet can quote every lyric from the latest rapper. They can recite lyrics that become destructive, self-fulfilling prophesies like, "I'm a thug," and, "I'm a gangster." There are kids in schools whose hip-hop hero is a literal murderer serving a life sentence! In the sixties, Dr. Martin Luther King Jr. wrote from jail about the social injustices that African-Americans were facing, and only forty years later, our African-American culture has become the social injustice itself. Hip-hop has helped to produce an environment where only 6 percent of African-American men go on to college and only 3 percent of them are graduating. Yet everyone is jumping on the hip-hop bandwagon, even equating it to the gospel message of Jesus Christ, in some circles. When will we wake up and take our God-ordained responsibility, declare war against this enemy, and give our youths the truth about what hip-hop really is? It's time to stop the dumbing down of this generation.

Pastor Theresa Goode, Youth Pastor
Jubilee Christian Church
Boston, Massachusetts

Chapter 18

Am I "Right" or "Racist"?

One dilemma I have encountered traveling and speaking to mixed congregations (Black/White/Hispanic) or all-white congregations is the concern they have for reaching out to the urban youths in their cities. There is a constant struggle by other races in reaching out to these so-called "hip-hoppers" in the communities surrounding them. But the dilemma comes when hip-hop is denounced by white pastors or youth ministers, because then, they are labeled racists! If they do not accept hip-hop into their youth groups or support the holy hip-hop movement by inviting hip-hop rappers and holy street thugs and gangsters to perform for their youth groups, they are labeled by the hip-hoppers as racists. When you speak out against hip-hop in any way in this country, you are automatically labeled insensitive to the movement and deemed a racist. Even when Black people speak out against hip-hop, they are considered sellouts by the hip-hop subculture. Bill Cosby, a famed actor/writer/comedian, who has overcome poverty to become a very wealthy entertainer in the secular world, was totally disowned by many in the Black community because of his outspoken comments against the hip-hop subculture. Here is what he said:

Bill Cosby: We Can't Blame White People

By BILL COSBY

They're standing on the corner, and they can't speak English. I can't even talk the way these people talk: "Why you ain't," "Where you is . . ." And I blamed the kid until I heard the mother talk. And then I heard the father talk. Everybody knows it's important to speak English except these knuckleheads. You can't be a doctor with that kind of crap coming out of your mouth. People marched and were hit in the face with rocks to get an education, and now we've got these knuckleheads walking around.

The lower economic people are not holding up their end in this deal. These people are not parenting. They are buying things for kids—$500 sneakers for what? And they won't spend $200 for Hooked on Phonics. I am talking about these people who cry when their son is standing there in an orange suit. Where were you when he was two? Where were you when he was twelve? Where were you when he was eighteen, and how come you didn't know that he had a pistol? And where is the father? People putting their clothes on backward—isn't that a sign of something gone wrong? People with their hats on backward, pants down around the crack—isn't that a sign of something, or are you waiting for Jesus to pull his pants up? Isn't it a sign of something when she has her dress all the way up and has all types of piercings going through her body? What part of Africa did this come from? We are not Africans. Those people are not Africans; they don't know a thing about Africa.

With names like Shaniqua, Taliqua, and Mohammed, and all of that crap, and all of them are in jail. Brown versus the Board of Education is no longer the white person's problem. We have got to take the neighborhood back. People used to be ashamed . . . [Today] a woman has eight children with eight different "husbands"—or men or whatever you call them now. We have millionaire football players who can't read. We have million-dollar basketball players who can't write two paragraphs. We as black folks have to do a better job. Someone working at Wal-Mart with seven kids, you are hurting us. We have to start holding each other to a higher standard. We cannot blame white people.

Sure, his statements were harsh, but were they true? And from where he is seated now, he looks insensitive to the movement, but where was "Coz" fifty years ago? In the ghetto! That's the part many forget. And because of the mentality of the hip-hop movement, if you don't celebrate the streets, then you aren't celebrating Black people because most of them are in the STREETS! I believe there is a sensitivity that we must all keep to the poor and poverty-stricken, but I also believe in placing a demand on everyone to DO BETTER! This comes with all of our help in teaching, mentoring, and filling in the gaps where lack is abundant. But this cannot come if we celebrate where they are! If a child grows up in the ghetto, and all he knows is the ghetto, then that is no cause for him to start a movement of "ghettoism" and begin celebrating the fact that he has a ghetto mentality. That child needs to be led out of the ghetto and into a place where he can excel and grow beyond his mentality because his mentality there is a culmination of his environment and his negative role models that dwell there among him. That's not to say that everything in the ghetto is negative, but I am saying that the ghetto is a symbol of poverty and lack, and if celebrated, then lack and poverty become the mark, and they don't overcome it all. Hip-hop has created a mentality that the streets are Lord, and you must respect them. For fear of losing touch with the streets, many try to stay true to the streets and celebrate what those in the streets respect. Gangs, violence, sex, greed, and immorality are celebrated in hip-hop, and the only real success stories in hip-hop are those that sell the very mentality that is destroying the rest of the hip-hop subculture! This makes it seem that the only way out of the poverty, lack, immorality, and ghetto mentality is the selling of it! If you sell this mentality to millions, you will get rich, while the rest get nothing! How selfish can you be? Hip-hop America is one of the most selfish groups of people because it's all about what you can get and the fastest way to get it. It doesn't matter how immoral it is; as long as you can make a profit, then sell it! That's the drug dealer mentality that once plagued many of our top-selling hip-hop artists; all they did was switch the product. But to me, drugs aren't as bad as the promotion and selling of immorality, self-as-god doctrines, and the love of money because all of these will lead you right back to illegal and defiant acts of selfishness.

Racist Double Standards

Since these things are so taboo to speak of in the Black communities by Blacks, without ridicule, I can only imagine what my white brothers and sisters are facing when deciding whether or not to embrace this subculture as a means of communicating effectively to their urban members and communities. If they don't accept it, they are labeled racists, but if they do accept it, they are being racists! Here is the bottom line: Hip-hop is an antichrist mentality that labels the white man as the devil and the Black man as his god. It makes blacks superior in every way to whites, and if you embrace hip-hop as a white youth leader or pastor, then you embrace the entire mentality that comes along with it. You must sit idle and accept the ignorant language, the inappropriate styles of dressing, hairstyles, and body art, and you must promote the street mentality because if you don't, you will be labeled a racist and one who stops the expression of the Black man! You see, hip-hop exists because the Black man felt that he could not effectively express himself due to the oppression of the white man, so if you go along with the hip-hop movement, then you cannot put boundaries on hip-hop's expression, or you will be guilty of the original "sins" of your fathers that birthed the movement in the first place.

But if you denounce hip-hop, then you can educate your lower-income youths and parents about the dangers of this mentality that is destroying youths. It must be done out of love, but with truth! You see, if you try to use hip-hop, then hip-hop will use YOU! You cannot accept a religion/subculture into your youth group that will promote the things that are not appropriate for your youths if you plan to ever help them. Your job is to create a counterculture, not promote a subculture. In other words, you are to promote Christianity that will surpass racial barriers and all cultural differences. But if you promote a subculture, you will have to minister to every subculture through their own means of understanding, which is solely based upon their environments and mentalities. That would be like a school having a white English class for rich white kids, a Mexican English class for Hispanics, and a ghetto English class for urban Black youths! All would be learning a different way of speaking English, but in essence, no one would be learning true English! The same goes with ministry. If you attempt to reach all subcultures through their own subcultures, then you will have to submit to the laws that govern their subcultures, whether good or bad. You will have to respect their mentalities and get down on their level just to speak effectively to them when the problem is their mentalities in the first place! If their belief is racist, then are you going to become a racist to reach them? If their language is profane, are you going to use profanity to reach them? When the apostle Paul said he would become all things to all men, he wasn't saying that he would submit to their beliefs, but he would supply their needs. We should never submit to the beliefs of a subculture to preach Christ. We don't have to! Christ sells Himself, and we cannot make Him any more attractive to a person than He makes Himself, no matter how we try to package Him. Promote Him and His ways, teachings, and words. If we show Jesus, we will offer Him to any culture or subculture without compromise. Remember, if you compromise Christ to win people to Him, then they will be accepting a "compromised" understanding of Him, and this will plague their walk with Him. Christ must be lifted up and shown for who He is. If that is done, then you will have no problem winning souls for Him, and you will be able to promote answers for those who are plagued by negativity and lack. You see, if you become the answer, then you fulfill the need. That's what Paul was saying. He would become the answer to all men, that he may win them, not further promote the problem! If you become the very thing that is plaguing the youth, then you are supporting the wrong side.

I know there is plenty confusion about using only the word "hip-hop" and not subscribing to the negative aspects of it, but let's be realistic. Can you use the word "Muslim" without subscribing to the beliefs of Islam? Can you use the letters "KKK" and delete the racism side of it? Can we change the orientation of the word "voodoo" and make it holy voodoo? When we use a word that carries a certain mind-set, connection to immorality, or negative stigmatization, it becomes synonymous with the definition of the word. Some try to reach the youth by using what they were used to doing in the world, but that is wrong, in most cases, because of why they were doing it in the first place. If it was sin that drew them to it in the world, and it was attractive to them because of how it agreed with their sin nature, then when they come into the church, it should be denounced, and a new mind-set should be taught and established to replace the negativity of what once ruled their understanding.

For white pastors and youth pastors, denouncing hip-hop is an even greater task because it will cause you to appear negligent in reaching out to the Black youth in your communities, but it's imperative that you stand firm and not allow yourself to be sucked into this paradigm shift in the church. Once you subscribe to hip-hop, you are accepting the spirit behind it all and also promoting the racist beliefs that are hidden in the mind-sets of the leaders of hip-hop. The white man is the devil, and the Black man is god to them, so in essence, you MUST comply with the order of hip-hop and the gods of hip-hop. If you choose to denounce it, according to KRS ONE and the other refiners of hip-hop, then you go against the original gods of this planet, the Black man! This is absurd, but it is righteous in hip-hop. This belief system is self-serving, self-centered, and self-minded in favor of the Black man and totally deletes the existence of Jesus Christ, who is deemed "the white man's God" by the hip-hop subculture. So it cannot be tolerated, used as a vehicle of ministry, or used as a platform for entertainment purposes. When you promote anything in your ministry under the title hip-hop, you are feeding the subculture and promoting its agenda. When you use hip-hop to reach hip-hoppers, you become an advocate for it and also join into the mind-set that hip-hop MUST be used to get them to God. It validates their belief that hip-hop is a valid religious belief and it is equal to and, in some cases, greater than God. Therefore, you can never use hip-hop without being used by hip-hop!

Chapter 19

What the Devil Feared About Me!
(And You, Too!)

I was lying in my bed one night, and all of a sudden, something came into my room. I remember looking at the ceiling and seeing a ball of light turning colors over and over again. It was so brilliant and full of awe that I could not look at it. I covered my face and began to weep. It was the presence of God! God spoke to me and said, "Come; I need to show you something." I remember being taken away, and my spirit was traveling with the Spirit of God. He took me around the world and showed me the nations. I could see the earth and the people in it. The Lord told me that I would speak to people globally, proclaiming the message of His kingdom.

God told me that someday, I would speak on His behalf. I was then taken back into my room and placed back into my body! I'll never forget it! God called me that way and confirmed everything that others had told me before. I knew I had to get focused on what He had for me. All of my past failures and pains seemed to no longer matter. Though God didn't cause my past pain and failures, I knew He was going to somehow use them for His purposes (see Romans 8:28). From that point on, I knew that I was called, and I could not go too far from God. I knew God had a plan for me, but it's something to behold when God visits you Himself and calls you with His own voice.

A few years later, I wish I could say that I was as focused as the Lord wanted, but I wasn't. But God sure has a way of getting our attention, doesn't He? He could have come to me in the dramatic way He did before, but He didn't. He could have used a burning bush, as He did with Moses, or He could have spoken to me from a whirling tornado, like He did with Job. But this time, He sent His messengers again to remind me of my calling, of all places, in a college dormitory!

I was dating a girl who was attending Texas Woman's University in Denton, Texas, and I just happened to go and visit her one weekend. She stayed in a dormitory with connecting bathrooms, and her friends lived next door to her. They were the youngest prayer warriors I had ever met. These powerful sisters loved to pray and have Bible studies. Now, honestly, at the time, I wasn't interested in praying or studying the Bible because I felt like I had too many other important things that I was into, especially that night. And plus, at the time, I was still carrying around some of the hurt from my earlier years, and womanizing was one of the ways it manifested. As I recall that night, just before our date, the girls next door asked me to join them in prayer. I was thinking to myself, *I don't want to get all spiritual right now; it'll mess up my plans for tonight* (if you know what I mean!). Nevertheless, I agreed and went next door for prayer. (My guilt from my holiness upbringing wouldn't let me turn down a prayer meeting, I guess!)

Anyway, the young ladies began to pray, and for a few minutes, they were praying for general things like the school, the student body, and so on. Hoping for a quick ending to the prayer meeting, I eventually closed my eyes and followed along. Moments later, when I opened my eyes, the three young ladies where gathered around me! One was bowing in front of me; the other two were at each side of me. Then, all of a sudden, they began speaking in tongues, which scared me. You may be wondering why I was afraid. Well, I was scared because I just knew the Holy Ghost was going to expose to them the plans I had for my girlfriend later that night! I thought, *Oh, no, I'm busted!* Yet, I felt like something deeper was about to happen. You see, God ruined my short-term plans for that evening to remind me of His long-term plan for my life!

One of the girls bowing in front of me began to interpret the tongues, and I'll never forget what she said. Here's part of it: "I have called you to take My message to the world. Just as this young lady bows before you, so shall men bow before you in honor of the calling that I have upon you. You are Mine, and I am with you!" The presence of God filled the room, and I could not believe what I was hearing! I didn't know what to say or do; all I could do was weep because I had heard what she was saying before. All my life, as the enemy tried to hurt and destroy me through sexual abuse by women in my church, the early loss of my father, being poor to the point of living out of my car, and being depressed to the point of attempting suicide, God sent people to alert me of His intentions.

Thank God for those who were obedient to His voice because I wanted to die, but through them, God said, "Live on!" I knew that God had called me, and now I was eager to see what He had in store. Little did I know, the pain I was experiencing growing up in Fort Worth, Texas, was familiar to the people that God was raising me up to speak to around the world: the hip-hop generation.

I began this chapter speaking of the visitation I had with the Lord as a teenager. I've come to realize that the encounter I had with the Holy Spirit that night is not about me, but about an encounter God wants to have with this generation. Whether you or someone you know is tired of living a life of sin, is depressed to the point of despair, or is struggling with the will to live, I'm living proof that if you give up your temporary pleasures for God's eternal purposes, God will reveal His plan for your life. What the devil fears most is when you first come to Christ. And what the powers of darkness fear most after salvation is your knowing God's plan for your life, and knowing the devil's strategy against you, and knowing God's desire to set this generation free.

This book is also meant to be a "wake-up" call to leaders. If you're a leader in the body of Christ, you don't need the encounter I had to know or confront what's happening to our youth. Let the statistics shared earlier be your bright light; let them be your burning bush; let them be your whirlwind that speaks to you. In other words, these stats represent the cry of a generation. Their need is your call to action, and now! And remember, we can't give up because when the enemy comes in like a flood, the Lord will raise up a standard. In the midst of depressing statistics and overwhelming odds, our God is speaking to this generation, "Live on!"

Chapter 20

Give Them the Truth

This is a real battle for our youth. It's a real battle to choose, at a young age, truth over your reputation amongst your peers. The youths of our nation are battling to be something in this life and are struggling to not be negatively influenced by the media, the hip-hop subculture, and now the church youth groups that embrace hip-hop. Our ministry is seeing thousands of youths come to Christ off the streets, out of the ghettos, and out of all kinds of sin struggles by receiving the gospel of Jesus and the message of truth. The Bible says this about truth:

> Howbeit when he, the Spirit of truth, is come, he will guide you into all truth: for he shall not speak of himself; but whatsoever he shall hear, that shall he speak: and he will shew you things to come.
>
> John 16:13 KJV

The Spirit of truth will testify of what the Father desires, not what man desires. When the truth is taught, plain and simply, it will cancel lies! Ultimately, when the lies are canceled, the true person is revealed. Hidden sins, low self-values, immorality, negative environments, broken homes, demonic self-as-god worship, and the hip-hop subculture will all be canceled out by the teachings of the truth. When a person receives the truth, the lie is evident, and a choice can then be made to follow one or the other. I believe that all truth should be taught to our youth about their lives and their upbringing, including mistakes that adults have made. I believe that the revealing of past mistakes that parents have made is the key to reaching out to the children—not music, or assimilating their trends, but remaining in a position of authority over them, yet being transparent about your own faults and errors.

I remember when my father died. This was the lowest point of my life. I felt abandoned by him and neglected by God. I knew he was going to die, yet I wanted him to live. When he died, I felt like I was in a dream world where the ground beneath me vanished, and I was walking on air. I had no sure footing. It really hurt me, and it made me question God about a lot of things. I remember one particular day, I was praying to God in anger, and I was saying things like, "If You are real, God, why didn't You answer my prayers concerning my father?" This went on for about a month, and then one day, I heard God speak to me. God spoke to me and told me that I was to pick up where my father left off. He said I was the continuation of my father, and everything he couldn't do, I was to do as if I were a spiritual extension of him. God then reminded me of the visions He gave me years earlier of me speaking all over the world to youths and parents. So I point blank asked God the question that was always in my heart: "God, what is the secret to reaching youths?" I heard the voice of God speak to me again, and He told me a very simple, yet complex, answer.

God said, "Your past!" God told me that if young people know where I came from and they see where I am in Him now, then they see hope! But if they never know that I was once like them and have made serious mistakes like they are making now, then I erase the hope of them ever being where I am because they can't see themselves at a starting point! In other words, whatever they are into or have done does not have to be their end if they see that I overcame my youthful errors. This was very powerful to me and changed my life forever. Yet, I wanted to see it in action. I'm the type that, if God said it, I want it proved by life and my actions. I don't want to just talk about it, but I want to live it. I remember asking God to show me what He meant.

At the time, I was teaching high school Gospel choir, and we were having a late evening rehearsal to prepare for a choir festival. I had about eighty kids in my choir at the time, but about twenty showed up that evening for the rehearsal. When we were in the choir room, we had just finished going over a song, and God spoke to me and said, "Tell them your testimony!" I remember stopping the music and asking the choir to sit down and listen for a minute. Then I told them that I needed to open something up to them about me because God led me to. Then I began to share with them my childhood story of how I was molested at a young age at my father's church and how that affected my life. I also told them how I was homeless at one point and living on the streets, in cars, and other places because of my anger toward my father. I shared it all, and when I finished, there was not a dry eye in the room. There were young girls and guys in there. Some of the guys were hard-core fellows (the gang type). They would be hard brothers walking the halls of the school, yet, in there, they were teary-eyed as well. There was a long pause, and then one girl got up and said, "I was gang-raped by five of my cousins when I was twelve years old, and since then, I have been sexually active and hooked on pornography!" Then, another girl stood up and said she had had two abortions and was only sixteen years old! Then a young boy stood up and said he was sixteen and had been a male prostitute and homosexual since he was fourteen years old and was molested by every pastor he tried to get help from! By then, the room was full of sobbing and weeping, but in the midst of it all, I heard God speak to me and say, "I can fix it!" No matter what they were saying and how bad it sounded, the Holy Spirit kept speaking in my ear, "I can fix it!" After everyone finished, I spoke to them the truth of the gospel of Jesus. I told them about the power of God and how He changed me and can change them. I preached to them for about fifteen minutes, and then we prayed. While we were praying, the power of God swept through the room, and deliverance began to take place. All the youths were being healed and set free, and my mind was being renewed about change.

You see, after my father died and after seeing so many youths around me lost to the subculture of hip-hop and the negativity of our society, I really began to believe that there wasn't much hope for our kids of this day. I felt that because they didn't have a good, strong home, because music and television were corrupting them, and because the subculture of hip-hop was training them up in idolatry and self-worship, there was no hope for them ever really getting free. But how wrong I was! God showed me that day that you don't need music, you don't need gimmicks, and you don't need to ever give them what they already have in the world! All they need is the truth and your testimony. When they see the change that has taken place in your life and hear you testify of how you once were, they see a path to their own freedom and deliverance. If we would get before God and allow Him to use us, we would not have to conjure up tantalizing methods of getting the youths' attention. But the truth of the gospel of Jesus will hold their attention once the truth is born in them!

After that night, the youths begged me to have a similar time again the following week. Needless to say, it grew into a weekly Bible study and, eventually, a citywide youth ministry! And the power of God would be so strong in our youth ministry that demons would be cast out every week. Young people would come from all over the city and totally change, all because His way was the way we chose, and because of it, many are being set free all over this world. Pastors, youth pastors, and youth leaders, I challenge you to listen to God and follow His direction when ministering to youths.

Don't give them what the world is offering them. Don't use the world as your model of effective attention-getting. Preach the Word of God to them and teach them. After all, whatever you give them is what they are going to expect the rest of their lives. So if all you have to offer them is hip-hop beats and worldly dances, then they are not going to be prepared for the adult worship when they come of age. But if you effectively teach them and challenge them to read the Bible, study the youth lessons, and witness, then you are setting a precedent that will benefit them for the rest of their lives. Many adults have problems reading the Bible and praying because we were not effectively taught it at a young age, so now it's hard for us to stay faithful to doing it. Well, if all we give our kids is entertainment, then what are they learning? Sure, we should have fun times in our youth groups, but we must never forget the real focus of their being in church. We must stop approaching them like they are only there because their parents are there. They are "the church" and must be taught how to function as blood-bought believers in these wicked and perilous times. Hip-hop is your enemy, so fight against it. Don't use hip-hop to describe anything you are doing for Christ or in your church because when you do, you are fulfilling prophecies spoken by the prophets of hip-hop, KRS ONE and Afrika Bambaataa! They claim that the only way to God is through hip-hop, but for us, as believers, that's Christ's place!

A missionary once told a story that illustrates this point. He was going to a remote village in the continent of Africa to preach the gospel, and had with him his translator and another person who was his guide. With compass in hand and machetes beating back the brush, he suddenly realized that the guide was not using a map. Nervous about getting to their destination, he mentioned his concern to his translator, who, as well, became alarmed. The translator spoke to the guide in their native language, and they both began to laugh. The missionary said, "What did he say?" The translator replied, "He said, 'I am the map. I am your trail. Follow me.'" You see, Jesus Christ is our guide to reach this generation, and we must follow the leading of His Spirit. He is the way! Follow Him!

"Jesus saith unto him, 'I am the way, the truth, and the life: no man cometh unto the Father, but by Me.'"

John 14:6

Appendix

Appendix A

Don't X Me Out

As we bring this to a close, I want to go through three things that are very important. I do not believe in just touching on these three things and not explaining them. I know in our churches, we have a lot of kids and a lot of teenagers who are given a stone instead of bread. What I mean by that is, they come to youth service, and all they are given is dancing and stepping. Now, let me say I do believe in having fun as a teenager; do not get me wrong. My teenage daughter has fun and I allow her some freedom in that, but I do not allow her to indulge in things that are going to be potentially dangerous, and more importantly, I have to balance it out and give her the truth of the Word as well. They have to know what being saved is all about. They have to know what baptism is all about, and what being filled with the Holy Spirit is going to do for them. These are things that aren't being talked about because a lot of our leadership is not filled with the Holy Spirit and a lot of our leadership is really not saved. So we have an issue here where our youth aren't getting the proper training in the areas that are able to make them strong and make them stand against the sin that's being promoted in their schools and in the media.

Celebrities

It's hard to get a mega church pastor to preach against the negativity promoted in the media. Why? Well, to be a mega church pastor, you have to use the media. It's hard to get a celebrity bishop to preach against the entertainment industry. Why? Because the entertainment industry is full of celebrities; the music industry and media are full of celebrities. So in order to be a celebrated person, you can't tear down what you desire to use to be lifted up. So you can't preach against the sin of Hollywood, what's being promoted on TV and so on, when you are positioning yourself to be great, lifted up, or celebrated, because it will hurt your opportunity to get in places where people will celebrate you. In the true church of God, men aren't celebrated. Now, I'm not saying, "Do not celebrate the accomplishments of others." Maybe give awards to someone in the church who's helped out; maybe even honor the pastor as the head of the church. I'm not talking against that. But I'm talking against being a celebrity where you mingle with Hollywood, compromise the truth about sin, and the world celebrates you! So I want to break down these three things for you before we close out this book so you can get a good understanding of what I am trying to show you. I desire you to know what true salvation is all about as well as the truth behind hip hop. So let me illustrate a few things for you so you know what I'm talking about when I say the basics, the 101, being saved, filled with the Holy Ghost, and being baptized.

Filled at Salvation

First salvation: 1 John 4:10 says, "Herein is love, not that we loved God, but that he loved us, and sent his Son to be the propitiation for our sins" (KJV). So, Jesus was sent to be sin for us, to stand in sin's place for us, to die as sin for us. In other words, anyone who sins is worthy of death. We need Jesus Christ to take away our sins, or become sin for us, so He paid the ultimate price of death for us. What did He do? He died on the cross to pay the price of sin so that any man who believes that he did and accepts Him is saved. Now, I know that inclusion says, "He just died for the sins of everyone, and they do not even have to accept Him," but that's a lie. The bible is clear that it takes accepting Christ as your savior, and receiving Him as your Lord to enter into eternal life. God requires us to change and he will shun those that do not desire to follow His plan. Inclusion is rising up because in this day, more and more homes are consisting of a mother and not a father. So, the disciplines that men stand for and exemplify are missing in the rearing of many of today's youth and adults. This brings about that "momma god" type complex that makes people desire to be nurtured by God rather than disciplined by God. Mothers nourish and are usually more lenient when it comes to disciplining the child versus a father who is a disciplinarian by nature and will usually hold a child accountable for his action when he is strong. So, when it comes to understanding our heavenly father, we need earthly fathers to be examples of discipline and accountability for one's actions. So, inclusion makes God more of a momma and causes the image of God to represent a nourisher rather than a disciplinarian. It's momma god saying, "I'll take you, baby. Whatever you're doing, baby, it does not matter, baby; I'm still your momma. It does not matter, baby; here I am." No discipline, no chastening, no, "Hey, if you do not accept Jesus, if you do not want to have it my way, then the devil is yours." Jesus even told them, "You are of your father the devil." "You were a murderer from the beginning; you are of your father the devil." So that means there are some who believe they are in, but they are really of the devil. He even said that everyone who says, "Lord, Lord" is not going to enter in. Those are the inclusionists that He is talking about. They are going to say, "Hey, I cast out devils in your name," and He is going to say, "Depart from Me; I do not know you." That's the Bible.

Romans 5:19 says, "For as by one man's disobedience many were made sinners" (KJV). He's talking about Adam. Because Adam disobeyed and brought sin into the world, many were made sinners. We are all born in sin and shaped in iniquity because of what Adam did. But the rest of that Scripture says, "So by the obedience of one shall many be made righteous." So because Jesus died for all of our sins, we are all able to become righteous in the sight of God if we accept what was done and if we accept forgiveness of our sins. Sure, we will make mistakes and we may fall at times, but this is why we need the grace of God. We have to have it because we are in a flesh world, where our flesh is tempted. And nowadays, when there are so many issues running prevalent in our lives—fatherlessness, homelessness, children being born out of lust instead of love, divorce, rape, molestation, all these issues that are plaguing this generation—because of these things, there has to be a period of grace, and God allows us to come to Him and get right. Yeah, we may fall and stumble, but we have to grow in it.

That's why you have to plug into a church where you are going to learn the truth of God, where you are going to learn about what it is you have received, because Romans 6:1 says, "What shall we say then? Shall we continue in sin, that grace may abound?" In other words, should we continue doing the things we were already doing just because there is grace? The Bible says, "God forbid" (v. 2). That means, God won't allow it! To forbid something means to not allow it. "God forbid. How shall we, that are dead to sin, live any longer therein?" (v. 2). In other words, if you are dead to sin, then how could you keep sinning? If God, in whom there is no sin, lives inside of you when you are saved, how could you keep sinning? What did you get saved for?

The Importance of Baptism

That brings me to my next point: baptism. Baptism is very important, and I'm not talking about a bunch of sprinkling and shaking water on somebody. I'm talking about submerging, being dunked in water. Every youth conference should be followed by baptism. At every youth service, they should be running water while the altar call is going on. We have got to get back to this because this is very important. Pay attention to this. Romans 6:3 says, "Do you not know that as many of us as were baptized into Christ Jesus were baptized into His death?" That means just as He died on the cross for sin, you died with Him also through baptism, to your sin. "Therefore we were buried with Him through baptism into death" (v. 4). In other words, going into the water represents your dying.

False Baptisms in Secret Societies

I'm going to tell you something. All of these different secret societies are smart enough to know that to get into them, there has to be blood oaths and death oaths taken. And they do not just take a death oath like in freemasonry, but you have to perform a ritualistic death to symbolize the oath in the natural realm. They will put you in a coffin, or they will cover your head and put a noose around your neck. They will do some form of ritual that symbolizes you dying so you can be born into their cult, born into that mind-set. The you that once existed is dead and the new you that is under their blood covenant is born. They know that's very important, and it puts a curse on your firstborn and the children who are born into your family after you perform one of these wicked death curse rituals. I talked about it in *The Truth Behind Hip-hop, Part 4: The Curse of the Culture.* That's where a lot of the death rituals have taken place and a lot of the death in the Black community. That's why our numbers are dropping population-wise, because of these death oaths.

These secret societies and organizations are just mimicking God's order of baptism. They know that when you are baptized, it symbolizes your death and rebirth. So when you go in the water, you are dead. But it says, "We were buried, therefore, with Him by baptism into death, so that as Christ was raised from the dead by the glory of the Father, we too might walk in newness of life. For if we have been united with Him in a death like His, we shall certainly be united with Him in a resurrection like His." In other words, as He died on the cross and rose from the grave, we symbolize our death with Him by being placed in the water and being submerged and pulled out. We come up a new man, with a new mind-set, and we believe this is very significant in salvation because it causes us to be dead with Him and rise with Him symbolically. And as children are to go back into their normal lives and go back into these schools and other places, there are so many things tempting them. But because the symbol of being reborn is there, they will always remember, "I went down with Christ, I rose with Christ, and now that makes me stronger." It's not a ritual, but it is something that was commanded by God for us to do.

The Power of Baptism

Listen to this: When we are baptized into Christ, we are baptized into His death, and therefore into His burial and resurrection as well. Through baptism, we are united with Christ in His death, burial, and resurrection. And being united with Him in this manner, we rise to new life, leaving behind our old self and rising to a new life. Baptism is when our old self dies and our new life begins. Baptism is when we stop living for ourselves and start living for Christ. Through baptism, we die to ourselves and exchange our life for His. Baptism is also when we come into contact with the blood of Christ. It is in baptism that we "die" with Christ, and therefore, we will live with Him as well. In other words, what happens in baptism is that God takes Christ's death, burial, and resurrection and transposes them onto our life. Our old, sinful self becomes united with Christ in His crucifixion and death through baptism, and we rise from the water to a new life.

This is why our kids are saying they are Christians, but are still doing the stuff they used to do. This is why our recording artists are saying they are Christians, but for twenty years, have still been hooked on pornography. This is why these things are happening and preachers are falling. People aren't being baptized and rising to a new life. Some folks were baptized when they were two, three, or four years old—they do not remember that! If this is the case for you, you've got to go and get baptized again. I know some people are going to disagree with this, but it has to be a memory that is prevalent and relevant in your life so you will know. You have been in sin all these years, and you say you were saved, but you were not saved. Go get saved and get baptized again and be raised out so that you remember you were raised with Christ. It's very significant to the new life that you're claiming you have in Him.

The Power of Being Filled With the Holy Ghost

Now, it doesn't matter how you say it, "Holy Spirit," or "Holy Ghost". I just say what the Bible says: "being filled with the Holy Ghost." There are a lot of fundamentalist teachers, especially holy hip-hoppers, who do not know anything about being filled. They know about the Spirit of God living in you once you have been saved, and that's important to know. But there is an empowerment of the Holy Ghost that comes upon you to give you power as well. Most people that do not believe in this power are those that have not received it. So I'm sorry if it hasn't happened to you, but it has happened to me.

I felt the fire of the Holy Ghost enter into my being. I have spoken with tongues in this experience. So we can play the "Well, tongues this and tongues that," but tongues are not the most important part of the experience of being filled. The issue is being empowered. Sure, the power of Christ comes in you when you accept Christ. But there is another infilling that comes upon you to empower you for certain things.

I remember when I first received the vision for *The Truth Behind Hip-hop*. When I first stood up in a church, I think it was in North Carolina, the power of God hit me in a way that made it hard to even stand up. It empowered me to preach a certain message, a message I hadn't studied, a message I hadn't researched, a message that just came spontaneously. And it was the power of God that came upon me. I was able to lay hands on sick people, and they were healed. I was able to cast devils out of people as well.

I know there are many doctrines that deny this power and if that's your belief, then I'm not putting your down, but I am in disagreement with your doubting. If you do not desire to be empowered then this message is not for you. I'm talking to people who want to be empowered, so they can stand against sin and lasciviousness. So they do not have to think they have to shake their butts to glorify God. So they can stop using the flesh as a scapegoat and an excuse for why they live perverse lives or why they listen to perverse music. I'm talking about folks who want to be filled with the power of God, to operate in the things of God. Those who want to help their neighborhoods, get people delivered, cast out devils, and heal the sick. I'm tired of seeing our young people crying out for help. They need the power of the Holy Ghost. Let's talk about this.

. . . Shall Come Upon You

Acts 1:8 says, "But ye shall receive power, after that the Holy Ghost is come upon you: and ye shall be witnesses unto me both in Jerusalem, and in all Judaea, and in Samaria, and unto the uttermost part of the earth" (KJV). Who is He talking about? He was talking to His disciples. Who are His disciples? I'm His disciple! I know they want to say, "Well, that was back then," "Well, if that was back then, then being saved was back then," "If that was back then, then being baptized was back then." Is the power of baptism still active? Is the power of salvation still active? Then why isn't the power of the Holy

Spirit still active? Why isn't the infilling still active? It isn't active in you because you do not believe in it! Don't act like the scribes and the Pharisees, questioning Jesus.

Listen, Acts 2:4 says, "And they were all filled with the Holy Ghost, and began to speak with other tongues, as the Spirit gave them utterance" (KJV). Why were they speaking in other tongues? God wanted the people of God to see the power of God in operation. That is the reason they spoke in tongues. And I believe in the speaking of tongues because it edifies you, according to what Scripture says. "Well, how does it edify me?" you ask. Because you are doing something that is supernatural. Anytime the power of God is operating through you supernaturally, it is edification to your spirit. It is proof that there is a power on you that is not of yourself.

That is why it is not by my ideas that I do this. It's not by my might that I do this. There is no way on earth that God could take a little boy from the country and put a message against hip-hop in him, and this message goes all over the world without tv or radio promotion, without retail sales, and not a dime spent on promotion. Not one DVD sent to ask, "Can I come and speak, preach, or minister?" Not one time, and this message is international. What is that? That's the power of the Holy Ghost! The people are not calling EX Ministries for music. People are not calling EX Ministries for entertainment. People are not calling EX Ministries to get the kids crunk so they can shake their butts. People are calling because there is a power in operation that is needed to sustain these children in this last day. We must be relevant in the spirit, not in the natural. We must cast out the devils that are plaguing the children in the spirit, not appease their flesh in the natural.

Listen to this; Matthew 10:19-20 says, "But when they deliver you up, take no thought how or what ye shall speak: for it shall be given you in that same hour what ye shall speak. For it is not ye that speak, but the Spirit of your Father which speaketh in you" (KJV). What spirit is He talking about? Is He talking about the spirit that comes in when you initially get saved? No, He's talking about the power of the Holy Ghost that comes upon you to empower you for a task. I remember for years, I would be in church and say, "Lord, fill me with the Holy Ghost. I want what I see. I want to be able to do . . ." But it was not until I gave everything to God and I decided that I was going to let the Spirit of God dwell in me and embody me so that I could be used to help somebody else, that the power of God came upon me—when I needed Him. When I needed power to preach the gospel and when I needed power to lay hands on the sick, the power was there.

Testimony in Detroit

A demon manifested in a girl when I was preaching in Detroit, Michigan, and because the church was so crowded, they brought her in the restroom for me to deal with. She was hollering out, folding over, and she was sick. She was crying out because of the demon in her. And the instant I went in there, the power of God filled me, and we were able to lay hands on her, and she coughed the demon up out of her! Something that had plagued her for many years, because of rape or molestation, came out of her. Now she is able to walk freely in the newness of life! What does the person that does not believe do in that situation? What do you do when someone has a demon, and you do not even believe in casting out demons? That girl would have gone home bound and sick because you had no answers for her?

Acts 4:8 says, "Then Peter, filled with the Holy Ghost, said unto them, . . ." What is this saying? What is this telling us? This goes back to Matthew 10:19, where it says, "Do not worry about what you are going to say, because in that instance, the Holy Ghost is going to come upon you and give you what to say and speak through you." And here we are, with Peter going before the council. There is another Scripture where Paul is going before the council, and the minute they get ready to open their mouths, what happens? The Bible says, "Being filled, that moment, with the Holy Ghost, they spoke what God wanted to say." That was the power of God in operation, and that is what we need.

When these kids go before that teacher or principal who is a lesbian at that school that's wicked, they can open their mouths, and the Holy Ghost will speak through them. When that boy tries to take advantage of that girl who is hurting, or when that girl tries to take advantage of that boy, at that moment, the Holy Ghost can speak through them. When a demon manifests in the lunch line, when a demon manifests on the school bus (I've got stories about this), the kids are able, at that moment, to be filled with the power of God and lay hands on people and make that situation okay. That's what our generation needs.

Suppressed Power

There is a power, but it's being suppressed by beats and rhymes. It's being suppressed by holy gangsters and holy thugs. What is going on, people of God? The only way these kids are going to make it is for them to be filled with this power of God. One more Scripture, Mark 16:17, says, "And these signs shall follow them that believe; in my name shall they cast out devils; they shall speak with new tongues; they shall take up serpents; and if they drink any deadly thing, it shall not hurt them; they shall lay hands on the sick, and they shall recover" (KJV). Who is he talking about? He's talking about people who are filled with the Holy Ghost, the power of God, to do the things that God would do. Jesus even said, "The things you see Me doing, the Father is doing." In other words, "Because My Father's Spirit is in Me, I'm able to do what My Father does."

Empowered to Resemble the Heavenly Father

But our generation does not have fathers, and so they do not know what it means to do or be like their fathers. A lot of their fathers are in prison, and they are doing what their fathers are doing. A lot of their fathers are no good, and they're doing what their fathers are doing. A lot of their fathers have taken death oaths in secret societies, and their kids are doing what they are doing. A lot of their fathers are homosexual, and they are doing what their fathers are doing. That's why God has to become the Father of this generation. The power of God has to dwell in them and the blood of Jesus has to cover them. The power of God has to fill them and they must take part in the death, burial, and resurrection by symbolically dying with Christ and being raised like Him! Be saved. Be baptized. Be filled with the Holy Ghost, so that you can stand in these last and evil days.

Appendix B

Yeah, But What About . . .?

This chapter is to help you understand the questions people raise about listening to the type of music that we have placed on this site. We are CD destroyers! People who don't want to give up their music, or people who just don't care enough to hear this message, constantly challenge us. You will be confronted with the same types of people. Here we have answers for their questions. The Bible states:

> But sanctify the Lord God in your hearts: and be ready always to give an answer to every man that asketh you a reason of the hope that is in you with meekness and fear.
>
> 1 Peter 3:15 KJV

ARGUMENT: I don't listen to the words; I just like the beats/music.

RESPONSE: Your subconscious records everything! You may try to block out the lyrics, but you cannot stop them from being recorded into your mind. Your mind can even record backwards messages. It has been scientifically proven that your mind is so clever that even when you aren't trying to, you can receive the information that is stated in the lyrics of music—even if it is recorded backwards! And it affects you! When you listen to sex, sex, sex, or murder, murder, murder, those are things that will come out of you in the heat of the moment. They are programmed in your mind without your consent.

PROOF: How many TV commercial jingles do you know? And how many of those did you actually learn purposely? Your answer is probably that you never intended to learn them, but because they played in your mind, you learned them without putting forth any effort. Now, where do you think the foul messages from hip-hop are going when you listen to them?

SCRIPTURE: Galatians 6:8: "For he that soweth to his flesh shall of the flesh reap corruption; but he that soweth to the Spirit shall of the Spirit reap life everlasting" (KJV).

ARGUMENT: I'm not influenced by music. I can listen to it, and it won't even affect me.

RESPONSE: Then why do advertisers pay up to $1 million for fifteen seconds of commercial time during the Super Bowl? They know something that you don't even know about yourself. They can play their commercial jingle and show you pictures of things, and influence you to buy their product in a matter of seconds. Your mouth gets watery, your lips get white, and your stomach starts growling because your hunger and your ears begin to work together to cause you to desire that hamburger! Well, the same goes for sin. Your fleshly man and those lyrics/videos begin to work together to cause you to desire sin. Our flesh is already wicked and desires things that are not of God. So what happens when you mix that with sinful lyrics or sinful video images?

PROOF: What kind of music do you like? Okay, now, what kinds of things do you do that are not of God? Told ya!

SCRIPTURE: James 1:14-15: "But every man is tempted, when he is drawn away of his own lust, and enticed. Then when lust hath conceived, it bringeth forth sin: and sin, when it is finished, bringeth forth death" (KJV).

ARGUMENT: The secular artists that I listen to are Christians. Even though their lyrics are foul and they dress provocatively, they say they are Christians.

RESPONSE: Who are they working for? You see, they have to be responsible for their actions. If they are making music that causes young people to sin or be tempted to sin, then they aren't working for Christ. If they use profanity, sex, drugs, violence, sexy costumes, or any other sinful thing to sell records, then they cannot be working for Christ. Therefore, if they aren't working with Him, then they are working against Him. Moreover, they are subject to the demonic forces that control the recording industry.

PROOF: Count the number of songs that glorify sin on one of this group's albums. Then, count the number of songs that glorify God on the album. Who won?

SCRIPTURE: Matthew 7:21: "Not every one that saith unto me, Lord, Lord, shall enter into the kingdom of heaven; but he that doeth the will of my Father which is in heaven" (KJV).

ARGUMENT: What is wrong with Gospel artists singing and recording with secular artists? That is a way to get the Gospel out to the sinners, right?

RESPONSE: Music was never used in the Bible to win the lost. Music was always used to prepare the hearts for the Word of God or the presence of God. Music cannot win a soul. When Paul and Silas were locked in jail, the Bible says that they sang praises to the Lord, and the doors opened. A guard heard them and fell to his knees and asked, "What must I do to be saved?" The music stopped, and Paul preached the Word to him! Yeah, a lot a people feel good after they hear the ONE Gospel song on these foul albums, but are they getting the Word afterwards? How can they when the next song is XXX content! You see, there is a deep danger in the spirit realm when Gospel artists record with sinful secular artists. You are opening people up and not completing the job.

However, the worst part is that the message of Christ is made a non-effect by the message of sin. You are causing people to sin, and then letting them know it's okay as long as they sing about Christ afterwards. God forbid. Music cannot save them. Look at Lucifer in heaven. He was making God's music and ushering in the very presence of God. But his heart turned evil and proud. Did the music change him? What about the sinful artists you are recording with? Is the music changing them? NO! They can record a twenty-song CD and have one Gospel song, and if it doesn't change them, what makes you think it will change others who listen to it? I have yet to hear one of these "crossover" Gospel artists say that the rest of the music on the secular albums that they are recording on is bad! They can't because they are on the project!

And what happens when Gospel music fans want to hear the new song that their favorite artist has recorded? They have to buy the sinful CD, and sit and listen to the sin, sex, violence, and so on, to get to the Gospel song. Do you know what you are doing to the youths of America? Not only are you supporting the secular industry, but you are causing Christians to buy the XXX CDs just to hear you! Can you imagine a fifteen-year-old Christian purchasing Missy Elliott's CD because they are a fan of evangelist Dorinda Clark's, or a fan of Yolanda Adams's? Can you imagine what happens to them when they listen to "Get Ur Freak On" or "One Minute Man" while they sleep or while they are riding in their car? God is upset, people! He would never tempt people with sin before He offers salvation!

PROOF: Imagine a large, twenty-four-by-twenty-four-foot billboard of two teenagers having sex. And on the bottom corner, written very small, are the words "Jesus Christ." Now, what do people see first? Why? Because the painting glorifies the sin, and not Christ. And even worse, Jesus' name appears as a signature of approval and not a message for change! Now, imagine that the billboard is a CD. Get the picture?

SCRIPTURES: Luke 11:23: "He that is not with me is against me: and he that gathereth not with me scattereth" (KJV); Ephesians 5:11: "And have no fellowship with the unfruitful works of darkness, but rather reprove them" (KJV); 2 Corinthians 4:2: "But have renounced the hidden things of dishonesty, not walking in craftiness, nor handling the word of God deceitfully; but by manifestation of the truth commending ourselves to every man's conscience in the sight of God" (KJV).

ARGUMENT: What's wrong with Gospel artists getting famous, making secular dollars, and signing contracts on secular labels? After all, the wealth of the wicked is laid up for the just, right?

RESPONSE: First of all, there is a price for fame. Jesus Himself didn't want to be famous because of what it would cost Him. That's why after He performed miracles, He would always say, "Don't tell anyone." Are we better than Christ, that we should seek fame? Should anyone carrying the name of Christ desire to have his name higher than His? Who are we glorifying, His name, or our name?

Second, signing a secular contract sells away your right to make your own decisions about your music. How can a person who is governed by secular ideas, marketing strategies, and demonic influences be in a position to hear from God? The record company has the final say! You have put yourself in a position to be governed by the enemy, and not God. Whatever they want from you, you are legally charged to give. Wherever they say to go, you must go. Whatever they say to do, you must do! All for the sake of fame and "getting out there." The saddest part is that the mentality of our nation's musicians is changing. Now, before they ever hear from God, before they even get seasoned or, many times, get saved, they are searching for a record deal and trying to "get out there."

Third, this Scripture has been taken out of context. The key to the whole Proverb is the phrase "laid up" or "set aside." That means that it is "detached" and stored up for the just. God is not going to use you to prosper the wicked! God is not going to use a Gospel artist to promote a sinful artist. He is not going to let you use His name to validate the lifestyle of a sinful artist! God forbid. If the wealth is still attached to the wicked, God doesn't want it. Since these wicked artists are hurting His people, they and their money are cursed, as long as it's attached to them. So don't use this Scripture if you are talking about money you are "making" for the wicked. God will lay it up, or set it aside, for you.

PROOF: Remember when Saul tried to keep the wealth of the wicked and offer it to God? (1 Samuel 15:2). God didn't want it because it was from the very people that were destroying His people! Or what about Achan! (Joshua 7:1). Was the wealth he kept "laid up" for the just? Well, the very people who are destroying the minds and hearts of our youths today are hip-hop artists! Do you think God wants you to make them prosper even more? God forbid!

SCRIPTURE: 1 Corinthians 10:20: "But I say, that the things which the Gentiles sacrifice, they sacrifice to devils, and not to God: and I would not that ye should have fellowship with devils" (KJV).

ARGUMENT: But I gotta have my music! What am I supposed to listen to? You are taking away the fun of living. Why can't we just stop being so picky about things?

RESPONSE: This thing is spiritual. If you are thinking naturally, you will never understand the message of EX! You will not understand what God really has for you. And you will not make it to heaven without being "spiritually minded." If you desire secular music, secular clubs, sinful movies, and sinful things all the time, you really need to check your lifestyle. Are you really saved? Has God really come in and changed you? Are you free from demons? Are you free from curses? Please, my friend, look into your life. Check it out.

What has happened in America is that the people with curses, demons, or serious emotional issues and problems are famous now. They are making the music that the world is buying. They are spreading confusion and the very hidden issues in their lives to the public. And people with issues love and desire to be with people with issues! Even in Gospel, artists with undealt with demons, emotional problems, and dysfunctions are famous now! And they are causing many others to follow them without even addressing the hidden issues of their own lives.

PROOF: Remember that Lucifer did not leave the presence of God alone, but he convinced one-third of the angels to follow him. How in the world can you convince anyone to leave the presence of God for evil? MUSIC!

SCRIPTURES (Read them all, thoroughly!):

Romans 8:5: "For they that are after the flesh do mind the things of the flesh; but they that are after the Spirit the things of the Spirit.

6 For to be carnally minded is death; but to be spiritually minded is life and peace.

7 Because the carnal mind is enmity against God: for it is not subject to the law of God, neither indeed can be.

8 So then they that are in the flesh cannot please God.

9 But ye are not in the flesh, but in the Spirit, if so be that the Spirit of God dwell in you. Now if any man have not the Spirit of Christ, he is none of his.

10 And if Christ be in you, the body is dead because of sin; but the Spirit is life because of righteousness.

11 But if the Spirit of him that raised up Jesus from the dead dwell in you, he that raised up Christ from the dead shall also quicken your mortal bodies by his Spirit that dwelleth in you.

12 Therefore, brethren, we are debtors, not to the flesh, to live after the flesh.

13 For if ye live after the flesh, ye shall die: but if ye through the Spirit do mortify the deeds of the body, ye shall live.

14 For as many as are led by the Spirit of God, they are the sons of God.

15 For ye have not received the spirit of bondage again to fear; but ye have received the Spirit of adoption, whereby we cry, Abba, Father.

16 The Spirit itself beareth witness with our spirit, that we are the children of God" (KJV).

ARGUMENT: Jesus ate with sinners and was around them all the time. That's how He reached them. Why can't these Gospel artists go to the world by recording with secular artists? What's the difference?

RESPONSE: Yes, Jesus did reach out to sinners to win them. He did eat and spend time with them. This argument had me stumped! I searched for an answer to this argument and couldn't seem to find one. But the Holy Spirit answered me very clearly one day. He told me to go to this Scripture, Ephesians 5:11: "And have no fellowship with the unfruitful works of darkness, but rather reprove them" (KJV). I still didn't understand the answer. But the Spirit spoke to me and said that the key to this verse is not the word "fellowship" because Jesus did fellowship with unbelievers. But the key is the word "works." The Lord asked me what BMI called a published song. A "work"! I was shocked. The Lord said that He indeed fellowshipped with sinners, but He never produced unfruitful "works" with them. When you record on a secular CD, you are a part of an unfruitful work of darkness. When Christian artists record on these sinful hip-hop albums, their intentions may be good, yet because the content of the rest of the CD is related to sex, drugs, and sin, the CD is an unfruitful "work" of darkness! If you call BMI and ask them about that CD, they will refer to it as a "work." And because of the sin, the CD is promoting the kingdom of "darkness," right? So is this the type of fellowship of an unfruitful work that the Lord was referring to? You bet! If it hurts the minds of people in any way, it is not a work of Christ.

PROOF: If you are riding in a car with someone, and he or she gets pulled over for having drugs in the car, guess who goes to jail? Even if you didn't know, you will go down because by riding with that person, you are saying, "I agree," or, "I condone your actions." People of God, when you record, listen to, or in any way support this hip-hop movement, you are in agreement with it fully. You are condoning by association!

SCRIPTURES:

2 Corinthians 6:14: "Be ye not unequally yoked together with unbelievers: for what fellowship hath righteousness with unrighteousness? and what communion hath light with darkness?

15 And what concord hath Christ with Belial? or what part hath he that believeth with an infidel?

16 And what agreement hath the temple of God with idols? for ye are the temple of the living God; as God hath

said, I will dwell in them, and walk in them; and I will be their God, and they shall be my people.

17 Wherefore come out from among them, and be ye separate, saith the Lord, and touch not the unclean thing; and I will receive you" (KJV).

ARGUMENT: God can still use the Gospel artists even though they are recording with secular artists, right?

RESPONSE: This is a very good question. Many feel that we are asking people to destroy their Gospel CDs as well as their secular CDs. But you have to be careful how you handle this information on our site. We own and enjoy Gospel music from certain artists who have recorded with secular artists. But we do not encourage the support of projects that are in support of secular artists. For example, we love Fred Hammond's project *Purpose by Design*, and we support his own projects because he doesn't use secular artists, nor does he use secular producers. However, we will not support his collaboration with P. Diddy on Bad Boy Records because we don't want our money to support the enemy's weapons against our nation's youths! We do believe that the "anointing" can be compromised and lost by these artists if they continue to compromise their integrity and join with these explicit artists in the name of Christ. Recording for and with these hip-hop artists says one thing and one thing only: that you are in agreement with them and what they do! Jesus never produced "works" with sinners. To do that, you must join with them spiritually and agree with their spiritual state. After all, if you disagree with their lifestyle and method of making money, how can you join with them to prosper them and help promote their cause?

PROOF: The Word of God was very clear in its dealings with the prophet Ezekiel and the sin of Israel. In the book of Ezekiel, God's people began to close their eyes to sin because of prosperity, and they began to teach and promote sin. The prophets and ministers began to join with prosperous sinners and began to embrace the sins of the people without standing up and teaching the true Word of God. They even began falsely prophesying to justify their actions. Sounds like our Gospel music industry. Homosexuality was ignored and not dealt with. Vanity and self-promotion were ignored and the norm. Mixing and mingling with sinful secular people who claimed God and yet worshiped idols and other gods was and still is an abomination to the living God! How can you join your ministry with that? So we do believe that good music can be created by many of these compromising artists, but you must allow God to lead you in your support of them. After all, Lucifer was allowed to make music in heaven, but when he crossed the line, he was removed. Many Gospel artists are crossing the line by supporting the secular industry, and it's up to us as a church to take a stand. So do not allow sinful secular artists, producers, and writers to prophesy their doctrines of sin upon your ears. Even though their lyrics may be Gospel, they are joined to Satan and are workers of iniquity! And since music carries their spirit, you may be inviting an evil presence into your church, into your home, or into your mind! God does not want any part of it. Check out what He told Ezekiel about this same subject in the Scripture below.

SCRIPTURE: Ezekiel 5:11: "Wherefore, as I live, saith the Lord GOD; Surely, because thou hast defiled my sanctuary with all thy detestable things, and with all thine abominations, therefore will I also diminish thee; neither shall mine eye spare, neither will I have any pity" (KJV).

ARGUMENT: If God is not working through hip-hop, how come so many people are touched by the music of holy hip-hop groups? They claim to be ministering in the Spirit and that hip-hop is their medium.

RESPONSE: A crowd of young people dancing and partying to beats and raps does not signify a move of God. The truth lies in, when the concert is over, whether they throw away the world's music. Are demons cast out of these youth? Do they want to change their lifestyle and live according to the Word of God? Holy hip-hop and any other form of hip-hop are not of God because of the spirit that operates through hip-hop. KRS ONE and others have been trying for years to get hip-hop in the church, and now they have through this holy hip-hop movement. That's why it's hard to even tell the difference between many of these holy hip-hoppers and the real hip-hoppers. Most of them dress the same, promote the same the spirits, and even imitate the real hip-hoppers while they are rapping. Youth pastors, pastors, and churches should beware. We must not allow hip-hop in our churches or allow it to be used to reach the youth. It's not necessary! Youth are YOUTH! They are attracted to beats and people who look like their worldly heroes. Even Kanye West was able to bring three hundred kids to the altar with his beats and lyrical style. Does that mean he was of God? Did the fruit remain? Was the Holy Ghost in operation? If what the holy hip-hoppers are saying is true, then we should just allow P. Diddy, Kanye West, and Jay-Z to start coming and ministering to our youth groups. After all, if hip-hop is a tool, then anyone can use it for good or for bad, right? We must not get this confused because the enemy wants the credit for everything that we do as Christians. If we say that we, as Christians, are holy hip-hoppers, then we are giving the credit for our way of living or rapping to the enemy because hip-hop rests upon his principles and doctrines, and not the leading of the Holy Spirit! If what we do is hip-hop in any way, then guess who gets the credit for it?

PROOF: Say you work for a major corporation like Sony. You come up with a monster invention that no one has ever seen before. You found a way to erase old CDs that you don't listen to anymore and re-record on them. You tell your boss, he gets the development team to build it, and it's placed on the market. From this point on, no one throws away CDs or sells them because they can now re-record on them. The world is changed by your invention. Who gets the credit for the change, you or Sony? Is your name on the invention? Is your face in the stores next to your invention? NO. Even though you came up with the concept, the origin of the idea belongs to Sony. Sony employed you, owned you, established you, gave you the resources, and even put you in the mode to create because Sony created the first CD!

Well, if what we are doing to reach the lost, win souls for Christ, and establish the kingdom of God is hip-hop, then who

217

gets the credit? God? No! The culture does because you have pledged your allegiance to the culture!

SCRIPTURE: Philippians 3:8: "Yea doubtless, and I count all things but loss for the excellency of the knowledge of Christ Jesus my Lord: for whom I have suffered the loss of all things, and do count them but dung, that I may win Christ" (KJV).

ARGUMENT: Isn't hip-hop just a culture, just as we have the American culture and the African culture? Many have said that the culture itself isn't bad; it's what's portrayed by the people in the culture that's bad.

RESPONSE: Let's be real for a minute. Cultures are subject to movements of people based on situations or circumstances surrounding them, right? That would mean that every culture has a base. And whatever that base is decides what the fruit of that culture will be. In other words, the roots determine the fruit! The roots of hip-hop are demonic. Oppression, anguish, poverty, violence, and other negative influences created this culture. Zulu customs, teachings, and ideals gave foundation and established the "positive" aspects of hip-hop. You must realize that God did not play a part in the creation, establishment, or foundation of hip-hop, so how can we drag Him into it at this late stage? KRS ONE says that he was visited by a spirit and the spirit influenced him to accept his calling in hip-hop. This was also stated by Afrika Bambaataa, who is the founding father of hip-hop. How can we embrace this culture when its origins are evil and demonic?

Many Christians are trying to hold on to their pasts by staying true to the culture and embracing it because that's where they came from. But Paul says that he counts all that he had attained as DOOKIE! That means that we must let go of who we were and move on in our new identity in Christ. God never intended for the Black man to be oppressed, poor, and discriminated against. And God seeks to deliver us out of that mentality that influenced us to act on our oppression. But He never wanted us to look within ourselves and find the answers, as the hip-hop leaders preach, but He wants us to look to Him and use His method, the Word of God, to break free from the curses of our oppressors.

PROOF: Why did God, when He changed the lives of Paul and Abraham, change their names? All through the Bible, God would always change the names of or give meaningful names to those that He called and used. Each name would preach a sermon in itself about the person's transformation process or intent for living. Well, if God has changed you, how can you hold on to your surroundings, your old ways, your old thought processes? You cannot! God also would take His people out of their environments, away from their friends and family, and move them into new lands. But those who held on to their old customs or cultures were left behind. Why? Because where we come from is not where God wants us to stay. Listen, my people, God is not concerned with our cultures. He wants to establish a place for us in the only true culture, and that is the kingdom of God!

SCRIPTURE: Philippians 3:13: "Brethren, I count not myself to have apprehended: but this one thing I do, forgetting those things which are behind, and reaching forth unto those things which are before" (KJV).

ARGUMENT: I heard a holy hip-hopper say that if hip-hop cannot be holy, then soccer cannot be a good sport because it originated as a form of brutal murder. Men's heads would be kicked around in medieval times, and that's where soccer originated. So do we not play soccer because its origins are corrupt? Well, even though hip-hop's origins are corrupt, can't we use it for fun, like soccer now?

RESPONSE: This is so ridiculous. First, people are not playing soccer with human heads anymore. There are no murderously bloody ones going on in our time. So it cannot be compared to hip-hop because the originators, the creators, the founders, and the evil hip-hop movement are still going strong now. Much stronger than the knockoff, "holy" version, will ever be. So the two cannot be compared. Secondly, soccer was not spiritual. No one in soccer is foolish enough to start calling it "good soccer" or "holy soccer"; it's just SOCCER. Only these rappers who want to do what their heroes of hip-hop have been doing are wanting to make the subculture/religion of hip-hop "holy." Real hip-hoppers know that it's just plain hip-hop. No holy version at all exists to them. To the streets, it's just hip-hop. And because of the demonic stronghold of hip-hop, God chooses not to join with it. Men may have ideas and plans, but the Spirit of God will not join with the spirit of darkness to get anything accomplished in the kingdom.

PROOF: This question is so ridiculous and unspiritual that I don't want to waste any more of my time proving it! If you want hip-hop, then follow the holy hip-hoppers. They will make you feel that you can be heaven-bound with your worldly identity. Hip-hop made you feel like somebody when you were in the world, so now you think you can join the holy hip-hop movement and keep those feelings with Christ stamped on it? Wake up, people.

SCRIPTURE: Galatians 5:1: "Stand fast therefore in the liberty wherewith Christ hath made us free, and be not entangled again with the yoke of bondage" (KJV).

ARGUMENT: You are not supposed to call names of people out in public like that. You are supposed to go to them in private first, right? How can you do that and call yourselves Christians?

RESPONSE: Our church is plagued with fear to expose the truth, when it's the truth that the Word says makes you free! We at EX Ministries may call out a few names of Christians who do things contrary to the teaching of Jesus in the church, and people think we are judging them. But the information we give is on the Internet, in magazines, and in other forms of media, yet, for some reason, when we repeat it, people call that judging and are ready to cut our throats! We are only bringing clarity to things that are said and done that are contrary to the Word! Isn't that our job? People act like it's OUR FAULT that some of the people we use as examples are doing the things they are doing against the truth. We receive vicious threats and profane e-mails every day from people defending various "Gospel" artists or ministers because of things that they, themselves, are doing that do not line up with Scripture. We are living in a sad day when people will fight to protect their favorite singers, rather than stand up for the truth of the Word of God. And whatever happened to that thing we used to have as saints of God called DISCERNMENT? I guess many are caught up in sin until they don't want anyone discerning them, so they cancel that ability as a saint. Check the Bible, people! Stating the truth is what Jesus taught us to do. Paul called out people publicly for what they did. Some to their faces (Peter in Galatians 2:14), and some he called out when they were not present to warn people of their contrary deeds (Hymenaeus and Alexander in 1 Timothy 1:20). Now, had their contrary deeds been done privately, then I'm sure Paul would have dealt with them privately. But when it's done openly, it requires open rebuke, according to the Word. So don't get disturbed when you hear that someone is doing something he shouldn't be doing. We are the body of Christ, and we are to keep each other lifted up when we fall. We are to keep the lines of the kingdom of God visible, according to the Word, and we are to keep guard that the enemy cannot infiltrate. Jesus said the gates of hell shall not prevail against the church. That means we must close off all doors or openings where the enemy seeks to enter into the church. Make sure you keep a good understanding about the Word, and know that we do not judge the world, but we have people that God has called to judge His people. Pastor, prophets, and so on are here to state truth and judge situations that require it in the church of God.

PROOF: Understand the Bible! Understand that people are going for TV, radio, movies, and more, and they are seeking fame. But when you are famous and you err on that level, then you must be corrected on that level. This is so that all who followed your error will be properly warned and can receive the truth of the matter. You see, many are making music, recording media (DVDs/CDs), and once this stuff is out, it's out! You can't take it back, and you cannot right all the wrongs because so many people were affected by the error. So this is why the Scripture tells us to confront before all in certain instances, because all need to know the truth of the matter. Don't get caught up in the hype. Many do not teach this because they are afraid of exposure. It doesn't seem right to our modern-day belief system because we live in a time when we don't like to expose the truth. We live in a time when people would rather be quiet and just allow the devil to run free without any warning. But if you are a true reader and believer of the Word, you know that EX Ministries' method of exposing truth is biblical and sound. Only those who do not read and understand the Word have a problem with it.

SCRIPTURE: 1 Timothy 5:20: "Those who continue in sin, rebuke in the presence of all, so that the rest also will be fearful of sinning" (NASB).

ARGUMENT: The Bible said, "Touch not My anointed," but you guys are talking against what bishops, pastors, and TBN are doing. These people are God's anointed, and you are in violation of the Scripture.

RESPONSE: First, let's take a look at what God was telling David when He made that statement. David was there to take Saul's life! He was going to kill him, but God said no. God did not want David to kill Saul because David was Saul's successor, and had David murdered Saul, David would have set a precedent of murdering leaders to take the thrown. God told him to "touch him not," but what He was saying was that He didn't want David to murder Saul. Yet, there are some obvious factors here that must be brought out to fully understand. It's obvious that David had already been discussing Saul's error to his men because they were there with him when he went to kill Saul. So David had already warned his people of Saul's error. Even though he loved Saul, he was prepared to kill him for the sake of right. He knew that Saul wasn't right, and he taught his men that Saul was not right. All throughout the Scripture, God raised up prophets, apostles, and leaders who exposed deceit and carnality in the body of Christ. There has to be judgment passed on believers based on their actions as well as their intent. Not eternal judgment, but judgment in the sense of sorting out the truth based on the Word of God. The Bible says that whether it be prophets or angels, if they teach contrary to the Word, let them be accursed!

PROOF: In 1 Corinthians 5, Paul judged a man based on his actions, and this man was not present! Paul called him out and asked for his removal from the church without his being present. What does this teach us? It teaches us that we do not judge the world, but we are judges of the body of Christ. We use discernment to look into things, and we use the Bible to "try every spirit," as the Word says. We go to our brother in secret when he sins secretly or discreetly. But we go to the public when heresy and public sins are committed. Don't try to use your flesh to understand this. You must be born of God and really a total Bible believer.

SCRIPTURE: 1 Timothy 5:20: "Those who continue in sin, rebuke in the presence of all, so that the rest also will be fearful of sinning" (NASB).

ARGUMENT: Shouldn't you just pray for these artists, and let God handle them? God should be the One who deals with them, right?

RESPONSE: Yes, we do pray. In fact, it was through years of fasting and prayer that God gave the revelation of this ministry! You see, how does God deal with men, according to the Scripture? WITH MEN! God uses men to deal with men. That's the problem with so much of our church these days. People don't want to be accountable to anyone, and they want to just pray about it and give it to God when God is trying to give it back to us to deal with. What is the pastor for? What is the prophet for? What is the apostle for? Come on, people! God uses men to deal with these issues and expose the lies in the body of Christ. God warns people through MEN. God speaks to people many times through MEN. God heals through MEN. God delivers through MEN. God created man to represent Him on earth.

PROOF: When God judged Pharaoh, He used Moses! When God judged Ahab and Jezebel, He used Elijah. When God judged David, He used Nathan. When God judged King Herod, He used John. When God judged the early church, He used Paul, Peter, and John. When God judged the Pharisees and the scribes, He used Jesus. When God judged Peter, He used Paul. And today, when God wants to rebuke, reprove, and expose, He will use

MEN. We can't just pray about it and get up, but we must pray about it and stay there until God tells us what to do about it! What if all these people I mentioned had said, "I'm going to give it to God in prayer and leave it there"? God is going to use MEN to carry out His orders, and there is nothing else to say about that!

SCRIPTURE: 2 Timothy 4:2-3: "Preach the word; be ready in season and out of season; reprove, rebuke, exhort, with great patience and instruction. For the time will come when they will not endure sound doctrine; but wanting to have their ears tickled, they will accumulate for themselves teachers in accordance to their own desires" (NASB).

Appendix C

An Interview with the author

"The devil is trying to erase lines that divide holiness from godlessness – and he's using hip hop to do it. So says G. Craige Lewis, founder of EX Ministries. Lewis is shouting from the rooftops about the Satan's strategy to infiltrate the Church of Jesus Christ with hip hop beats that are nothing less than demonic. Lewis has produced DVD series including, "The Truth Behind Hip Hop" that he says is corrupting praise and worship in the Church and "What Every Church Needs to Know About Hip Hop." He's also produced DVDs that expose, "The Truth Behind Abortion" and "The Truth Behind Rock and Roll." *The Voice* caught up with Lewis to draw from his 15 years of reaching out to those that have been led astray by our cultures embracing of evil and perversions and also to attack the enemy's invasion of the media and music."

Q. What is the root of hip hop music and why is it so wicked?
A. *If you trace Hip Hop back to it's conception, you will see that it has never been a music genre. Most people are surprised to learn that more than a music art form, hip-hop is a way of life. As one of its founders says, "Rap is what you do, hip-hop is what you live." Hip Hop is wicked because it is a subculture influenced by false religious beliefs from the Universal Zulu Nation, Nation of Islam, 5 Percent Nation of Gods and Earths, Rastafarianism, and other religions, and believes that the Black man is god and denies*

the supremacy of Jesus Christ as the only way to eternal life. Of course, we know that this mixture is in error, because Jesus said He alone is the way, the truth and the life, and know one comes to the Father, except through Him. (John14:6). To Hip Hop's founders, Jesus Christ is either one of many gods, or is just a prophet, or is just the White man's God used to oppress Black people, not the Son of God. Like all subcultures, Hip Hop tears away or deconstructs mainstream culture. This subculture that was birthed out of lack and oppression began to express those feelings more and more, essentially becoming the sounding board or platform for elicit speech and anti-establishment teachings against American society. Hip Hop celebrated being distinctly different from society, and saw rejection of the mainstream as a vehicle to obtaining a street credibility to earn the right to speak or be a voice for the "hood." Rap music was a genre and the art of rapping was basically rhyming to a beat with a poetic flow. However, Hip Hop is a street subculture that used rap to convey a language, a lifestyle, and a total street related way of thinking and behaving.

Before long, Hip Hop's spiritually mixed, self absorbed, self-empowerment "positive" message changed. As the streets became wicked and the heart of those in the streets became full of violence and rejection, so did Hip Hop. Rap music began to change and takeon the characteristics of the subculture of Hip Hop, thus, the rappers began to celebrate street life and their lack became their prize. In other words, when rap became about Hip Hop, then rap music began to promote the evils of the street, (pimping, hustling, cussing, slanging crack, etc.). It became a good thing to be a product of the streets and the street life began to be portrayed as the desired "way of life" because the music promoted it. This is a subculture and not a true culture because it takes the ideals of the parent culture of America and deconstructs them to form a group of people that are in America, but have a modified understanding and interpretation of the language, dress, and behaviors of American citizens that seeks to be set apart and have its own distinct identity. And because Hip Hop encompasses the street language and the negativity of deconstructed ideals, it becomes dangerous to those that buy into it. Sure, the leaders of every subculture profit because they are the leaders of a following, however, those that are not leading suffer the consequences of being separated from the American culture.

As a result, they are rejected by mainstream society when it comes to making the grade, getting a job, and fitting into the mold that is deemed "acceptable" by American society.

For example, well known hip hop artist that have black racist philosophies, sagging pants and tattoos are paid to look the way they do, but their followers who emulate them will not make it in society. You see, the devil makes the leaders rich, to keep the followers rejected by society, unable to function in the mainstream society and impoverished.

Q. How did you get this revelation about hip hop?

A. God revealed this stuff to me in a vision many years ago. I saw it all happening just as it is happening now. I talk about it in depth in my first video and I still share the vision on my website and when I speak. It was a powerful vision because we wrote it all down almost 20 years before it ever happened.

Q. So all hip hop is bad, then, right, no matter what the lyrics say?

A. Hip Hop has no lyrics. Hip Hop is not music, instead, it's a subculture that uses rap music to spread its ideologies. If you listen to any real Hip Hopper, they will tell you that Hip Hop is not music, it's a way of life. They say that rap is something we do, but Hip Hop is something we live. And if it's a way of life, then it is self expression. If it's self expression then it is a way to convey a message through a lifestyle. Isn't that essentially what Christ is, or rather, what Christianity is suppose to be? The other subgroup in a culture, is a counterculture, and Christianity is a counterculture which transforms us so that we don't have to express ourselves; Rather, we express Christ. The church doesn't have to model a street thug, gangster, or even have street credibility at all.

We model Christ. So, your question about Hip Hop must be answered like this: Rap is just a form of conveying a message like singing. Nothing is wrong with that. But Hip Hop is a lifestyle expressing one's self through a street subculture that was birthed out of lack and a deficit in the home. There was something wrong with it from the beginning. In Hip Hop's inception, people were poor, so they celebrated lack to feel better about poverty. It's like eating pig feet. Let me explain.

My race of people, African Americans, as slaves, were once forced to eat pig feet because that was the worst of the pig. Even today, many people eat pig feet. Does that make pig's feet good for you? NO. It's still as bad as when it was only food for slaves. The popularity of it does not change the fact that it is terrible for your body and has no nutritional value.

You see, it's the same with Hip Hop. It was created in the streets as a way to celebrate lack and having a deficit in life. Children without fathers in the home and those that lived in severe poverty would get together on the streets and have rap battles and such. The clothes they wore, (Dickie's and handed down attire) became the "in" thing to wear because that's all they had. way they spoke (broken English and slang) became their language because they didn't obtain quality education. The way they behaved, walked, and carried themselves became their identity, because they didn't have fathers to mold them or model, so they used the streets as their guide. Now, we want to take what the streets taught them and bring it into arenas where there are better examples of living, better language and communication skills to be learned, and better role models to follow and ignore the fact that Hip Hop is a street subculture? Why not end Hip Hop once you leave the streets? Why not forsake what the streets taught you when there is a better way?

We must realize that music is just a vehicle being used by those that prosper off this subculture to forward their money-making agenda. So, Hip Hop is just like pig's feet. No matter how popular eating it gets, it's still slave's food and terrible for you.

Q. Is it the beats, the culture, what is the issue?

A. *The issue is the consequence of buying into a subculture that hinders your forward progress in society. When you submit yourself to the ideal of a subculture that has set itself against the establish-*

ment, you heap pain and discouragement upon your life and immobilize yourself from being prosperous in the parent culture. You see, If the parent culture views saggin, grillz, broken English, earrings, corn rows, etc. as deviant behaviors, then you are labeled by the parent culture as a deviant. And because the American culture has the jobs and the Hip Hop subculture only prospers the leaders, then your average Hip Hop subcultural "wanna be" is without hope. When you are labeled deviant, you are judged by your appearance, language, and demeanor and left out from achieving any real success in the parent culture. In Hip Hop's worldview, the only way to "make it," is to engage in behavior which the dominant culture deems illegal or illicit: sell drugs, or escape reality by indulging in sex and drugs. As a result, while hip hop artists may rap about these things, their followers are led by these pied pipers to the only place where sagging, tattoos, black racists philosophies and corn rows are embraced: Prison.

Q. What would you say to proponents of so-called 'holy hip hop' who would argue this music reaches our youth in the name of Christ?
A. *Music reaches everyone. It's not a surprise that a gangster for God will have an audience just like a gangster for the streets will have followers. Mass murderers in prison have cult followers and many of them believe it's a godly following, but does that make it valid? The validity of it has to come from the Word of God and in my bible music was never used by God as a tool to spread the gospel message. Music has the power of coercion and can influence a person to feel changed when they are not. This is dangerous because people have emotional experiences and believe they are spiritual experiences. Music can make you feel good, bad, happy, sad, and people take this for God's power when in essence, it's just a feeling.*

This is why in the bible music was only used to bring Glory to God and never to win a soul. When a soul is drawn to music, it is soulish and fleshly. A person cannot make a valid choice for God under the influence of music because they are making a decision at that point based on feeling rather than a knowledgeable, informed decision with their mind and heart versus their emotions. Emotional decisions blow with the wind, but informed heart and mind decisions are based upon understanding and last longer.

God does not take subcultures and make them holy, he takes people. He takes prostitutes everyday and saves them, sets them free and makes them holy! He takes drug addicts and crack addicts everyday, saves them, and makes them holy. Those that belong to the red-light subculture, the goth subculture, the drug subculture, the hippy subculture, the gay/lesbian subculture, and the streetwalking subculture are saved, set free and delivered, never returning to the way of life they were delivered from. But when he makes them holy, are they still what they once were? Are the prostitutes "Holy Hoe's?" Are the drug addicts "Holy Crack Heads?" Are Hindus, "Holy Hindus?" Or are they new creations? They will be new creations that will not resemble their old ways, and are ex-pimps, ex- gangsters and ex- hip-hoppers. Once they have been transformed by the renewing of their mind, they no longer think, act or desire to look like what they were delivered from. It is called repentance, (see Acts 3:19)! Once God has changed our minds, we change our ways, and turn the opposite direction. Gospel Gangsta's, Preachin Pimps, and Holy Hip-hoppers are not new creations, but they are spiritual mutations that retain portions of who they were and thus, are flawed. They are not new, but just amended. They are not hot, but luke warm, a mixture of hot and cold. This is exactly what God said he will spew out of His mouth: Those that desire the world and God, (Revelation 3:16). The roots of hip-hop subculture are demonic, and are similar to other subcultures with an antiestablishment, "Down with the man" mentality.

Fatherless-ness, rebellion, oppression, anguish, poverty, violence, and other negative influences created this subculture. Zulu customs, Black Muslim teachings and other false religions established the so-called "positive" aspects of hip hop. Thugs, gangs, drugs, sexual promiscuity and prison life make up the other overtly dark facets of hip-hop. You must realize that God did not play a part in the creation, establishing, or foundation of hip-hop, so how can we drag him into it at this late stage? When KRS-ONE and Afrika Bambaata say they were visited by a spirit and the spirit influenced them to accept their callings into hip-hop, how can we embrace this subculture when it's origins are evil, demonic and destructive to society?

Q. Is there anything positive about so-called holy hip hop?
A. *I believe that most holy hip hoppers want to do good, but they also want to hold on to the world and what they rode through their own personal storms with them. Most of them didn't have fathers in the home growing up, so they gravitated to Hip Hop for identity, purpose, and fulfillment. This became a father like figure, so when they turned to Christ, they wanted to bring their "father" into knowledge of Christ with them. This is why they want to sanctify Hip Hop and make it holy because it's the only father many of them know. That is the biggest problem we face as black people: the lack of fathers. If there is no earthly father in the home, children have a harder time receiving the heavenly father once they come to the knowledge of him. So, they want God to be mamma instead of father. Mamma will allow things that father won't because of the emotional nature of a women. This causes many of these rappers to figure God will allow certain things, even though they are not scripture, because of their love and desire for these things. That's a "mamma god" mentality. Momma will allow it in many cases when fathers won't because of her emotional sensitivity to the child. But just because they want it, and because many desire it, it does not make any of it right. Hip Hop is a street subculture that has no place in God's church.*

Q. Just to be clear for our readers, is Gospel rap and holy hip hop the same thing? Or is there room for rapped lyrics in some instances?
A. *Rap is an art form that is comprised of rhythm and poetry. Preachers have done it for years. Children have learned fundamentals from it for years. It's a way of conveying large amounts of lyrics in short times for memory purposes and enjoyment. That is not essentially a bad thing. But Hip Hop is not rap. I believe a person can rap a song about Jesus and entertain others without it being Hip Hop, so long as they don't emulate hip hop lifestyles or images or attempt to emulate leaders within the subculture. The problem I see*

is that many Holy Hip Hoppers will never be content with calling themselves Gospel Rappers. Unfortunately, they need and desire the validation of Hip Hop to feel legit and have street credibility. You see, if you are subject to the streets by being apart of the subculture, then you need the streets validation, right? They can't just rap for Jesus. They have to look the look, walk the walk, talk the talk, and do what the real hip hoppers do. Hip Hop must be their way of life. What they don't understand is that you don't change hip hop, hip hop only changes you!

Q. I've heard you say hip hop causes youth to worship the devil. Can you expound upon that?

A. *Knowledge of self. Hip Hop rest upon the teachings of it's original founders who submit to the doctrine of the Zulu Nation and the 5% nation which teaches false god doctrine. KRS-ONE, and others teach these things and Hip Hoppers consider him the true prophet of Hip Hop. Even Holy Hip Hoppers pay tribute to the founders and consider them leaders and moguls. False god worship is devil worship.*

Q. Why and in what ways does music have so much power?

A. *Music can do what regular speaking cannot. It can bypass the frontal lobe of your mind and enter your brain without your consent. It bypasses your "guardian," so to speak, and influences you without your knowledge or your permission. That's why you remember so many TV jingles, and marketing companies know this and spend millions on them to influence what you buy. Because music can affect your subconscious without your permission, it gives music crazy power and makes it a dangerous thing in the wrong hands. That's why we should glorify God in our music and never use music to bring glory to ourselves. Music that glorifies God draws us to Him; unfortunately, music that glorifies self draws people to you and makes them worshippers of you. This is why we have people with celebrity mindsets even in the church. They are doing exactly what Lucifer did in heaven and that is making fans and followers that chase their talent rather than follow the God that they sing about. The bible says that their mouths draw close, but their hearts* *are far from Him, (Isaiah 29:13). This same principal can also refer to how you can sing God's praises and yet draw people to yourself. When music is used in this manner it's dangerous.*

Q. How has the devil managed to infiltrate the church with concepts like 'holy hip hop'? Where's the deception? Where's the cracks?

A. *Well, the devil just made the church folks worldly. Years ago, you didn't have to worry about anything like Holy Hip Hop coming into the church because people practiced sanctification from the world and didn't desire to bring the world into the church. But when Kirk Franklin came on the scene, he brought the club dances and worldliness into the church and made it okay to dance, party, and gyrate sexually without rebuke. Then you bring in bishops like TD Jakes who put on megafest and other conferences, with the worldly artists and performers headlining, and you have turned what was once deemed worldly into something that is now necessary to draw crowds and sell product. These 2 men, I feel, are responsible for the downfall of worship in the black church as a whole. Kirk destroyed Gospel Music as we knew it and made songs with secular overtones and worldly dances the norm, while TD Jakes turned preaching into an art form and totally removed the anointed call of God from the resume of black pastors all over. They both made it okay to be in the world and of the world. They crept in unaware and have removed the sacred landmarks of God's word and now the world looks at the church as a money making, powerless, group of folks that desire pleasure as much as they do. Those are the 2 cracks that Hip hop and every other worldly movement crept in through.*

Q. What's the hidden message in the hip hop culture?

A. *Hip Hop doesn't hide anything. The message is clear in the behavior, the music, and the appearance of Hip Hoppers. Love yourself and do what you want. Don't let the church, God, or man stop you. Do what you feel and do what makes you feel good. That's Hip hop's theme and the current that drives our millennium youth that are apart of it.*

Q. What does hip hop music ultimately lead to?

A. *Self worship. People that suffer for lack of validation and desire to be seen and known can find what they are looking for in Hip Hop because it causes you to practice self absorption all day, everyday. The beats satisfy your flesh. The lyrics lead and guide you to flesh gratification. The artists give you fleshly fashions and things to mimic so that you can get the looks and attention that they possess, while all along they are getting paid and the people that mimic them are lowering their chance of success. Since Hip Hop came on the scene in 1980, black men went from having 180,000 imprisoned to now over 1million black men imprisoned. Also, our crime rate has tripled. 50% of all black teens have genital herpes now. 1,400 abortions occur everyday in the black community. Our young black boys have a 75% drop out rate. And this is what is supposed to reach our youth, Hip Hop? Before there ever was Hip Hop, we were better. Hip Hop is a pied piper that led a generation into sexual immorality, false god religions, death and hell.*

Q. How can parents get through to their kids about this?

A. *Research. Get informed on what these folks are saying and doing. Don't just sit back and allow a Gangsta for God rap show to happen at your church or youth function but research it and don't tolerate it. Most of the youth pastor's that are bringing these Holy Hip Hoppers to their churches are uninformed, or they are fans. But a father or mother that is raising their child to be successful in America cannot afford to allow a street subculture to influence their child. Don't let anyone force you to allow this, but take action and fight against it.*

If it's allowed at your church then that speaks volumes about the leadership that you serve under. I can't think of any real man that would want the streets to be celebrated in his ministry or church. The church is supposed to get the streets out of people and get them in position to progress, not regress. How can you take care of your family and be an upstanding man, when you are carrying yourself like a street thug and gangster? You can't. Parents, wake up!

Q. How can we conquer this demonic weapon that's infiltrated the Church?

A. *If church folks would stand up and say "no more," then weak youth pastors and worldly pastors as a whole would reconsider supporting this movement. It's a money movement and when the money is not there, the movement stops. If you stop buying the cd's, the folks will stop making them. If you stop supporting the movement, the folks will find something else to move to. Plain and simple, the only way to stop Hip Hop is to shut it down financially.*

When secular Hip Hop is dead, guess what happens to Holy Hip Hop! That's why God is never relevant, but always absolute. He never chases the world's ideals, but he always creates his own. Why? Because the grass withereth, and the flower fadeth, but the Word of God will always stand, (Isaiah 40:8). The word is never contingent upon what the world is doing, but it always counters the world. We must follow God and not the world because the world will change, but God stays the same.

1. Rapture—the catching up of believers by Christ at the time of His return. Holman Bible Dictionary © 1991 Holman Bible Publishers.
2. Anti-Christ—a future Roman ruler who will appear during the tribulation and will rule over the earth. Holman Bible Dictionary © 1991 Holman Bible Publishers.